TRIUMPH
BOOKS

GOOD AS GOLD

GOOD AS GOLD
My Eight Decades in Baseball

Jim Kaat
with Douglas Lyons

Library of Congress Cataloging-in-Publication Data
Names: Kaat, Jim, author. | Lyons, Douglas B., author.
Title: Good as gold: my eight decades in baseball / Jim Kaat with Douglas B. Lyons.
Description: Chicago, Illinois: Triumph Books, [2022] | Summary: "A former baseball pitcher and current announcer, Jim Kaat reflects on baseball and his life"—Provided by publisher.
Identifiers: LCCN 2021056673 (print) | LCCN 2021056674 (ebook) | ISBN 9781629379357 (hardcover) | ISBN 9781637270271 (epub)
Subjects: LCSH: Kaat, Jim. | Baseball players—United States—Biography. | Pitchers (Baseball)—United States—Biography. | Sportscasters—United States—Biography. | Baseball—United States—History—20th century. | Baseball—United States—History—21st century. | BISAC: SPORTS & RECREATION / Baseball / General | BIOGRAPHY & AUTOBIOG-RAPHY / Sports
Classification: LCC GV865.K22 A3 2021 (print) | LCC GV865.K22 (ebook) | DDC 796.357092 [B]—dc23
LC record available at https://lccn.loc.gov/2021056673
LC ebook record available at https://lccn.loc.gov/2021056674

This book is available in quantity at special discounts for your group or organization. For further information, contact:
    Triumph Books LLC
    814 North Franklin Street
    Chicago, Illinois 60610
    (312) 337-0747
    www.triumphbooks.com

Printed in U.S.A.

ISBN: 978-1-62937-935-7

Design by Sue Knopf

All photos courtesy of Jim Kaat unless otherwise indicated

This book is dedicated to my daughter Jill,
who was diagnosed with stage four neuroendocrine cancer
about the time I started writing this book.
She passed away on March 5, 2021
from neuroendocrine tumors.
My proceeds from this book will be passed on
to the Neuroendocrine Tumor Research Foundation (NETRF).
Jill's attitude and resilience in handling this horrific disease
has been an inspiration to me.
And to my many baseball friends, colleagues, and teammates
who have left us in 2020 and 2021.

Contents

Foreword

I guess I first saw Jim Kaat sometime in the early '60s, pitching for the Minnesota Twins against the New York Yankees on WPIX Channel 11 in New York. A rarity in baseball in those days, the Yanks televised the vast majority of their games, and growing up on Long Island, I watched nearly every one. I met Kitty in 1982. His long and winding big league career had taken him to my adopted hometown of St. Louis, where he helped the Cardinals win the '82 World Series. In our initial conversation, I recalled a 1967 game at the old Yankee Stadium, where Jim had the Yanks shut out, leading 1–0 with two out and nobody on in the bottom of the ninth. The hitter was Mickey Mantle, nearing the end of his career, hobbled and fading, but still dangerous, especially from the right side. These days, I am apt to forget where I left my glasses or keys, but back then, I remembered distinctly that the count was 3–1, and rather than walk him, Jim threw Mantle a fastball that caught too much of the plate. The ghost of greatness blasted it over the 457' sign in left-center, a sector of the ballpark reached only a handful of times in its history. The shutout and the lead were now gone.

At that point, I obviously didn't know Jim well, but he seemed a genial sort, so I was guessing he would not be put off by the implied invitation to relive the moment. Not only was I right about that, but Jim, a baseball man to his core, was genuinely pleased and engaged that a kid like me—I was 30 but looked about half that—would be so invested in a long-ago game, in which he and Mantle were the central figures. He told me that while Mickey Mantle was, well, Mickey Mantle, Elston Howard, who waited on deck, had been an equally tough out for him. (I checked: prior to the homer, Mantle had been 0 for his last 5 against Kaat. Howard had doubled in his previous at-bat that night.) So Kitty didn't want to face Ellie with a man on and the game on the line. He figured he would take his chances with Mantle, and unless he hit it down the line, the cavernous ballpark would hold it.

No such luck. But a lucky encounter for me, as Jim and I had hit it off right then. We both recalled that after the homer, with the ballpark and both dugouts still buzzing, Howard followed with a single up the middle. Jim then got the third out. Extra innings. But then came a heavy rain—a rain that would not stop. The game was called and went into the books as a 1–1 tie. A fateful turn of events—because when the Twins returned to New York later that summer, Jim started the makeup game and was outdueled 1–0 by Steve Barber. The '67

Twins lost the pennant to the Boston Red Sox by one game. That one pitch to Mantle made a huge difference.

As it turned out, that random conversation between two baseball guys began what is now a nearly 40-year friendship, a friendship that became a professional partnership when Jim and I both joined the Major League Baseball Network at its inception in 2009. It was natural for us to be paired in the booth. Viewers tell us they can sense the ease and connection between us. It sounds like an ongoing conversation between friends, they say. And that's what it is: friends who share a lifelong love of the game. I have talked baseball with countless players, managers, and other baseball figures from old-timers to present-day stars. Very few are in Jim's league as baseball raconteurs. His vast knowledge of the game and its colorful personalities; his still keen insights; and his firsthand experience over more than 60 consecutive years in the majors as player, coach, and broadcaster are a hard combination to match.

Credibility? Two hundred eighty-three wins. Three 20-win seasons, topped by 25 victories for the Twins in 1966. Sixteen Gold Gloves. And for good measure, 16 home runs as a hitter. All this spread over 25 seasons from 1959 to 1983. He was 44 when he threw his last big league pitch.

How much of baseball history does Jim Kaat span? I often kid him that you can connect him to Abner Doubleday in about three moves. Instead, let's try it this way: Jim faced Ted Williams, whose career began in 1939. He also faced Julio Franco, who lasted in the majors until 2007. A 68-year link right there. But wait: several currently active pitchers, including Adam Wainwright, Jon Lester, and Andrew Miller, faced Franco. Ted Lyons, the White Sox Hall of Famer, began his career in 1923. He faced, among other immortals, Ty Cobb, whose rookie year was 1905. He pitched in the American League into the 1940s and thus faced Williams many times. So there you have it: Cobb to Lyons to Williams to Kaat to Franco to Wainwright. Virtually the entire modern history of baseball in five moves.

No matter how you express it, Jim Kaat has been an admired and enduring citizen of the game. What follows is the story of a good portion of a remarkable baseball life.

—Bob Costas

Introduction

I am one of the few people alive who can truly say that virtually every dollar I have earned as an adult has been because of my involvement in the game of baseball, a game I have loved since 1945, when I was about seven years old. Of course, I had multiple jobs as a teenager because fathers at the time encouraged their young sons to "go get a job" as soon as they could. As a teenager I stocked shelves and bagged groceries in a grocery store, sold clothes in Boonstra's clothing store, swept floors in Tony Last Hardware store, and washed dishes at Bosch's restaurant.

Even after I was a major leaguer in the early 1960s, I supplemented my income by doing some appearances and commercials for Cloverleaf Creamery in Minneapolis. In the first few years of my professional career, I announced high school football and basketball games for KSMM and KRSI in Minneapolis and I hosted some coaches' shows. I had to because ballplayers at the time weren't paid very much.

I am grateful that I have been blessed with the ability to play the game, coach the pitching part of the game, and for the last 35 years, to be a television analyst talking about the game I love more than any other. (I love golf too, but that's just a hobby.) I want to be perfectly clear that I have loved the special feeling the game of baseball has given me since 1945. Even today there is no topic that gives me more joy than sitting around with friends like Bill Parcells and Bryant Gumbel and playing baseball trivia or just talkin' baseball.

But baseball has changed so much. And in many cases, in my opinion, not for the better. The appeal of the game is still the ability of the players—at a higher level than ever before. There's more power and greater skill, agility, and speed. But it has decreased, in my opinion, in executing the fundamentals and in exhibiting in many cases a lower baseball IQ.

Pete Rose, the all-time hits leader, did not have much power, speed, agility, or even a strong throwing arm. But he was one of the greatest players of all time. Why? His baseball IQ—the anticipation, the ability to see the whole field, knowing what *every* player needed to do, not just what *he* needed to do. Rose, the ultimate team player, played more than 500 games at five different positions: first base, second base, third base, left field, and right field. He could play according to the scoreboard. What inning is it? What's the score? What's the count? Who's pitching? Who's batting? How many outs? Those things dictated what a player should do in those situations. Not so much anymore. Keith Hernandez and Derek Jeter used to be great at that. Hernandez was my teammate with the St. Louis Cardinals from 1980 to 1982. You could see him thinking at first base. Jeter knew where he was and what was happening around him on every pitch.

Mathematics says it's hard to bunch two or three hits together, so let's just swing hard in case we hit it. A higher percentage of at-bats result in a walk, strikeout, or home run. Is that what fans want to see? Why does it take more than three hours to complete a nine-inning, 2–1 game? That is an insult to baseball fans. I will discuss how the science, analytics, and metrics have ruined the enjoyment of the game for me and many fans of my era. There are loads of examples. Baseball has deviated from the original purpose of creating a relaxing entertainment on a warm spring afternoon. It has been replaced with promotional days to attract fans because the game apparently isn't enough to attract them. For example, loud music and players wearing their uniforms like they're dressed in pajamas. You don't have to lean on the past, but honor it and respect it—more so in baseball than in any other sport. Arrogance; the owners' greed; marketing every second on television and radio; the electronic scoreboards; odd starting times to get higher ratings when it is not an ideal time to play; too many night games even in the postseason, making it hard for kids to stay up late to develop a love for the game.

Again, let me be clear: this is *not* a criticism of today's *players*. They can be so entertaining with all the skills they possess. Why ruin that by turning them into robotic individuals? They deserve to display their intuitive skills without being influenced by the people upstairs on their computers. Roger Angell, the iconic essayist for *The New Yorker* and an avid baseball fan, recently turned 100. He made an insightful point: "I am not a numbers guy. The game is so hard, the players are so distant from us in talent. The numbers try to shorten that distance and make us really think we know what's going on down there on the field. They're really not very appealing to me."

My playing career ended over 35 years ago, and I am so distant in talent level from today's players that it looked like I was pitching in slow motion compared to today's pitchers. I'm 83 as I write this. I am concerned about the game being appealing to young fans in years to come. I hope I am wrong. A lot of people follow the game or follow their team, but they watch highlight shows to actually see it.

Here is an analogy, and I don't know if it plays. I resigned from the prestigious Medalist Golf Club in Hobe Sound, Florida, years ago because Greg Norman kept changing the design of the course. A hundred of us resigned because we would say after four or five holes, "Wow, this used to be so good. Now it's just ordinary."

Truth be known, many pitchers are unhappy with all the shifting by infielders. My friend and longtime manager Buck

Showalter and many other former managers and baseball people have an idea: two infielders required on each side of second base and at least one foot on the dirt by every infielder. I like it!

Television production screens are often filled with graphics that are really not pertinent or interesting and they aren't up long enough to read and understand, but our eyes are directed to them, and we take our eyes off the real attractions: the players.

I was fortunate to be a member of the 1982 Cardinals. We won the World Series. We hit 67 home runs and stole 200 bases. We played great defense and were an exciting team to watch. I wish today's fans could have seen that team play. There is a lot more to exciting baseball than titanic home runs. The 1998 New York Yankees were the most complete team in the past 25 years. They played the game the way it was designed. They executed fundamentals such as advancing runners, creating productive outs; they hit well with two strikes; and they hit a lot of sacrifice flies. The 1998 Yankees won 114 games and 11 more in postseason play. Tino Martinez led them in home runs with 28. They were a joy to watch play, and I was fortunate to have a great vantage point from the television broadcast booth wherever they were playing.

It was embarrassing for the Yankees in Game Two of the 2020 American League Division Series when their analytics people thought it would be good to start young righty Deivi García to get the Tampa Bay Rays to have all their left-handed hitters in their lineup and then bring in lefty J.A. Happ in the second inning. That ploy didn't work out well. The Yankees of Ruth, Joe D., Mickey, and Jeter turned to analytics to win a postseason game—and against the team which virtually invented the use of the opener. So sad. Postseason baseball is a separate season. Players react differently to the pressure. There is overthinking, overanalyzing, overtrying, and overmanaging. Just fill in the lineup card and let them play.

I have been passionate about the game since the mid-1940s. I have a framed piece of the box scores of the doubleheader I saw on June 26, 1946. As the years have gone by—and believe me, the older one gets, the faster they pass—I appreciate more and more the era in which I was born and raised. Over these eight decades, the game has changed so much. And in many cases, in my view, not for the better.

I had 463 teammates, including 13 future Hall of Famers: Catfish Hunter, Ron Santo, Mike Schmidt, Bert Blyleven, Goose Gossage, Rod Carew, Reggie Jackson, Harmon Killebrew, Steve Carlton, Ted Simmons, Gaylord Perry, Bruce Sutter, and Ozzie Smith. When I played my last game with the Cardinals on July 1, 1983, I had pitched in the majors 25 years—longer than anyone else in the 20th century. Bowie Kuhn, the commissioner of baseball, gave me a plaque commemorating that record. That record has since been surpassed by Nolan Ryan (27 years) and Tommy John (26 years) and equaled by Rickey Henderson, Jamie Moyer, and Charlie Hough. Hall of Fame second baseman Eddie Collins also played for 25 seasons. I hadn't retired. I was released by the Cardinals.

When Rose became the manager of the Cincinnati Reds in 1984, he asked me to be the Reds' pitching coach. I enjoyed my time as the Reds pitching coach from 1984 to 1985, but becoming a baseball analyst was a great opportunity for a second career for me at 46, so I left coaching after the 1985 season and I am now in my 35th year as a TV analyst. It turned out to be a good decision. I got to announce Yankees games in 1986 on WPIX-TV, their local station, where I worked with Bill White and Phil Rizzuto. Bill was a great mentor to me. Scooter kept me on my toes. Then I spent six seasons announcing Minnesota Twins games from 1988 to 1993 on WCCO and the Midwest Sports Network. I was an analyst on *Baseball Tonight* on ESPN in 1994 before the opportunity to begin a 12-year stint covering the Yankees on the MSG Network (1995–2001) and the Yankee-owned YES network (2001–06).

I still do some Twins games for Bally Sports North. In 1987 I did Atlanta Braves games on TBS. From 1987 to 1989, I did spring training specials and college games on ESPN. In

1988 I covered baseball (then a demonstration sport) at the Seoul Olympics for NBC television. From 1988 to 1993, I broadcast games with Dick Bremer and Ted Robinson for my old team, the Twins, on WCCO and the MSN, the Midwest Sports Network. From 1990 to 1993, I did nationally televised games for CBS with Dick Stockton and Greg Gumbel. In 1994 I did some major league games for *MLB Tonight* on ESPN. From 1995 to 2001, I broadcast Yankees games on MSG. From 1997 to 2006, Ken Singleton and I broadcast Yankees games on MSG and YES. Starting in 2009 and through today, I do showcase games with Bob Costas on the MLB Network.

I have changed since I started in the minor leagues in 1957 with the Superior (Nebraska) Senators in the Nebraska State League. So has baseball. My dad was an avid baseball fan and a Philadelphia Athletics fan because of manager Connie Mack and Hall of Fame pitcher Lefty Grove. John Kaat's interest in baseball shaped my life. My introduction to Major League Baseball started in 1945. It was actually because of small-town gambling. My dad bought a 5-cent token for me for the seventh game of the 1945 World Series (Chicago Cubs vs. Detroit Tigers) pool at Bosch's, a local restaurant in Zeeland, Michigan, where I was born and grew up. In small letters on the little circular wooden token, it said "DET. 5 1st." It meant that if the Tigers scored five in the first inning, I would win the pool. They did, and I got over $7 worth of nickels. That was a lot of money (the equivalent of about $101 today) for a seven-year-old kid in 1945.

The real motivation to be a player came on Wednesday, June 26, 1946. My dad took me to Briggs Stadium in Detroit, about 154 miles from our home in Zeeland, to see a doubleheader between the eventual pennant-winning Boston Red Sox and the Tigers. I remember it like it happened this year. When broadcasting for the MSG network in the late '90s, our pregame host, Deb Kaufman, asked if I would do a pregame interview when we were in Detroit about the first games I saw as a seven-year-old boy. During the interview I mentioned the scores of the games, the attendance, who hit home runs, who the pitchers were, and that the uniforms were the whitest white and the grass was the brightest green I'd ever seen. My friend and noted statistican, Peter Hirdt, heard the interview and said, "Oh yeah, those players *think* they remember things like that, but most of the time they're wrong." I was right on all counts.

I have been blessed to be a part of Major League Baseball for 62 seasons in eight different decades. I have met and made friendships with thousands of people. I'm writing this book to share the experiences I had as a player, coach, and announcer that spanned eight decades. I also share what I enjoyed about the game as a fan, player, observer, and announcer and what I don't like about today's game. I have a wish list that will never happen, but I hope it gives you an idea of how simple and enjoyable the game was for me as a boy and a player and now why it has lost some of its charm and appeal. This book is about the experiences I had as a player, coach, and TV analyst and the changes I've seen in the game for the good and the bad.

CHAPTER 1
The 1950s

I am the youngest of four children. I don't think my parents expected me. My oldest sister, Mildred, was 13, Esther was 11, and my brother, Bill, was eight when I was on born November 7, 1938. I was born at home in Zeeland, Michigan, a small town in southwestern Michigan not far from the shore of Lake Michigan. Its 2018 population was just 5,564. My sisters always knew when it was 4:00 PM because the whistle signaling the end of the work day at the Mead Johnson chemical plant blew loud and clear. The plant was right up Main Street from our house. Our house was also the home of East Limits Dairy, which my Dad owned and operated.

The Chicago Cubs, Chicago White Sox, Detroit Tigers, and Milwaukee Braves were all within reach of our radio signal in Southwest Michigan, and I loved listening to their games.

Basketball was a popular high school sport, and I enjoyed it at Zeeland High and did quite well at it. As a 5'10" guard, I won All-Conference and All-County honors. I could dribble, pass, and defend the other team's best scorer.

I was a trading card collector. Like most of my friends, I kept the prize cards in between the spokes of my bicycle's wheels. I have a feeling I had a lot of valuable cards in those spokes, like maybe a few early '50s Mickey Mantle cards. I enjoyed trying to collect starting lineups. The Philadelphia A's were my favorite team, probably because they were my dad's favorite. I had the cards of my boyhood idol, Bobby Shantz, and Ferris Fain, Eddie Joost, Pete Suder, Gus Zernial, and many others. I collected the Philadelphia Phillies, too, because they went to the 1950 World Series. They were called the Whiz Kids and were young and talented. Many of them became friends. Richie Ashburn, a batting champion and speedy outfielder, became a Hall of Famer. Robin Roberts, a perennial 20-game winner and future Hall of Famer, catcher Andy Seminick, and infielder Granny Hamner all became part of my life when I met all of them in 1976 as a member of the Phillies. One of my favorite wins as a pitcher was when I hooked up with Roberts in the early '60s when he was with the Baltimore Orioles.

I learned to score the town league softball games when I was younger than 10 years old. I scored some of the games I listened to on the radio as a boy. Then when I began broadcasting, it was a big deal to score games. I found that sometimes my broadcast partner was so interested in getting the play down in his scorebook that he stopped looking at the play on the field even when the ball was still live. One time I had to tap a partner on the shoulder to look up because there was a wild throw from the outfield, and players were running around the bases. As I got more into my broadcast career, we had stat guys sitting with us in the booth, and they kept score. I think keeping score is a good thing for a *spectator* to do but not a *broadcaster*. I like to keep my eyes on the field. If you are writing, you might miss something.

Just 18 miles from Zeeland was Moline, Michigan, where Frank "Stubby" Overmire, a 5'7" lefty who had pitched in the majors for 10 years, was from. He had a relative who was a neighbor of my Uncle John in Grand Rapids, just 21 miles away. Stubby visited Grand Rapids when I was about 11, and Uncle John arranged for him to visit me in Zeeland. Stubby gave me one of his gloves. I wish I still had it.

My baseball interest really got stronger when I watched the 1955 World Series, which featured Sandy Amoros' famous catch in left field on a drive by Yogi Berra in Game Seven and Johnny Podres' performance in Game Seven pitching the Brooklyn Dodgers to the championship. The next year had Don Larsen's perfect game in 1956. I became a fan of the Milwaukee Braves when they moved there from Boston in 1953. Milwaukee is only 97 miles from Zeeland. Detroit was about 175 miles away. I loved Hank Aaron, Warren Spahn, and Lew Burdette. I cut Burdette's picture out of my *Sport* magazine and taped it to my bedroom wall. He led the Braves to victory in the 1957 World Series and won three games in the '58 Series.

The '50s were life-changing for me. I went from being just a fan to a fan *and* a professional baseball player. Because the chicken industry was very big in Zeeland, my Zeeland High School team was called The Chix. After pitching for three years at Zeeland High, I pitched for the Hope College Flying Dutchmen for one season. We had a 12-game season. My roommate, Al Kober, pitched half of them, and I pitched the other half. They were all doubleheaders of seven innings each.

Dick Weincek, a scout for the Washington Senators, attended the doubleheader we were playing against Kalamazoo College. He came to see the Kalamazoo pitcher. I had a good game. Actually, I won all six of my games and only gave up a couple runs in all six games. I say that not to boast but to point out the difference in the game then and now. I didn't have a 95-mph fastball. But I did have good control, change of speeds, and movement on my fastball. Weincek was impressed enough to come watch me pitch the next week against Alma College. Jim Northrup, a future star for the Tigers, was on that team. I had another good game and then came the call to try out with the Senators when they came to Chicago a few weeks later. I pitched a side session to veteran catcher (and future teammate) Ed Fitz Gerald as manager Harry "Cookie"

Lavagetto watched. "Kid, you sign with us, you'll be on my staff in two years," he said.

On the ride home, I was obviously pretty excited about Lavagetto's prediction. My dad, drawing slowly on his corncob pipe, said, "Well, he may say that to a lot of young pitchers to give them hope." John Kaat always kept things in perspective and on an even keel.

I first met Senators legend Harmon Killebrew in spring training in Orlando in 1958. He, though, was not yet an established star with the Senators. Killebrew had been signed in 1954 as a bonus baby, 11 years before the draft was instituted. Previously, a team with plenty of money (read: the New York Yankees) could just sign any prospect they wanted, pay him as much (or as little) as they chose, and stash him in the minor leagues to prevent another team from signing him. To prevent this, the bonus baby rule was instituted in the major leagues. The rule was that if a player received a signing bonus and salary of more than $4,000, he'd have to be put on the team's 25-man major league roster for two years. This rule delayed the rise to stardom of Sandy Koufax and Killebrew. Some bonus babies like Paul Pettit, Paul Giel, and Hawk Taylor—the list goes on and on—never became productive major leaguers. Each ballclub was allowed no more than two bonus babies. My friend Ralph Lumenti had been a teammate of mine on the 1960 Charleston Senators in the Triple A

American Association. He got a $35,000 bonus, which is approximately $306,000 in 2020 dollars. Lumenti looked and threw like Koufax, but he sat on the Washington Senators' bullpen bench for two seasons and never developed into a big league pitcher.

Killebrew, who had awesome power, signed for more than $30,000. So he was forced to occupy a spot on the Senators' roster. It took him several years to finally become a star. (Over his 22-year career, Killebrew hit more than 40 home runs eight times, hit a total of 573 roundtrippers, and was inducted into the Hall of Fame in 1984.) Killebrew was one of the reasons my dad convinced me to take the $4,000 signing bonus from the Senators rather than the $25,000 which the White Sox had offered. I would go to Class D ball in the minor leagues and work my way up to the majors.

My dad had the foresight to know that I couldn't make much improvement sitting on the bullpen bench for two years. My dad was a more than avid baseball fan and knew the history of the bonus babies. So when Pete Milito, the area scout for the White Sox, called and said he thought the White Sox would offer me a contract of $25,000 because he thought I'd be in the big leagues in two years, my dad said, "Thanks, but Jim is going to sign for $4,000 with the Washington Senators and go to the minor leagues to learn his craft."

For perspective, my dad earned $72 a week at that time. I later did the math and figured that was less than $4,000 per year. So John Kaat gave up six years' salary so his son could learn to play the game from the bottom up. Guess what: I was called up to the majors two years and six weeks after I signed in 1957!

Killebrew had some lean years at the beginning of his career. By the mid-1960s, when he became the face of the Minnesota Twins, it was apparent that he was a special power hitter and a special individual who was powerful but polite and humble. We were teammates from 1959 to 1973 and remained close friends until he passed away on May 17, 2011. I was honored to be asked to speak at a memorial service which the Twins held for him at Target Field. We spent 16 years as teammates and close friends with the same organization. With free agency that doesn't happen much these days. Killebrew was one of the finest gentlemen I ever knew.

One of the highlights of my career occurred on June 17, 1957, when I signed my first professional contract to play for the Senators. I spent my first season as a professional ballplayer pitching for the Superior (Nebraska) Senators in the Nebraska State League in 1957. Despite a mediocre year in the Nebraska State League—I went 5–6 and an ERA well over 3.00—I considered it a great learning experience. I got knocked around quite a bit for the first time as a pitcher. The guys I faced were also the best coming out of their towns and schools. I had enough dominant games that when I returned to Zeeland after the season I told my dad that I wasn't intimidated. I could compete with these guys.

My manager was Ray Baker, a mean-spirited, profane, cigarette-smoking man who belittled us but had a soft spot somewhere inside him. He met with each player on the last bus ride home. His words to me were: "Kid, if you come up with a good fastball, you got a chance." Can you imagine a manager telling a kid that today? You have to have what scouts call a plus-fastball to even get drafted.

So in 1958 I found a fastball. I also grew from 6'3" to 6'5"and went from 180 pounds to 215 without any particular workout or diet program. It was just natural growth. That year was important because it was an example of how fragile a career can be and how thin the margin is between making it or not. I was added to the roster of the Class B Fox Cities Foxes in Appleton, Wisconsin, in the III League. In the '50s there were class D, C, B, Single A, Double A, Triple A, and then The Show. The Foxes were managed by Pete Suder, a former second baseman with the Athletics, my favorite team as a young boy. I had several of his trading cards or bubble gum cards as we called them. There was a piece of stiff, stale, break-your-teeth gum in every pack of five trading cards.

And then Jack McKeon entered my life for the first time. McKeon was the player/manager of the Missoula (Montana) Timberjacks in the Pioneer League. It was a Class C league with teams in Montana and Idaho. McKeon must have seen something in my ability because he approached me one day in Fernandina Beach, Florida, our minor league training site. He said, "Kid, if you come pitch for me, I'll be your catcher and I think I could help you develop as a pitcher."

Nothing against Suder, but this made sense to me. I went to see Joe Haynes, a former major league pitcher and team executive, and explained my thinking. He was all in for it. I became one of his favorites. He was a great supporter of mine during my early years. So I headed to Missoula with McKeon and 15 other players. Among my new teammates were Sandy Valdespino, who later became my teammate on the Twins and a good friend for many years, and Jay Ward, with whom I later played on the Twins. We had a seven-man pitching staff. Starters pitched every four days. They didn't count pitches then or restrict innings. They counted outs. The goal was to get 27 of them and pitch nine innings. For my first five starts, I wasn't doing much of either one. My record was 1–4 with a high ERA. If I didn't start pitching better, my next stop wouldn't be Fox Cities. It would be back to Zeeland to find a job. Here is what McKeon did for me which other managers might not have done. He met with me one day and said, "Jim, you're going to be a big league pitcher. You're going to start every four days. So just relax, and I think you'll pitch the way you're capable of pitching."

An enormous weight had been lifted from my shoulders. I ended the season 16–9 and led the league in almost every pitching category. The bosses even came to Missoula to see me pitch a game. I threw a shutout and struck out 13 against the Idaho Falls Russets. The bosses told McKeon after the game: "He pitched well, but I don't think he's got the stuff to make it in the big leagues."

McKeon challenged them with a bet about steak dinners and cash that they were wrong. McKeon is 91 now as I'm 83, and I call him occasionally at his home in Elon, North Carolina, and never fail to thank him for what he did for me.

Another highlight of the '50s was the bus rides. At 18 and 19 years of age, I wasn't exposed to the pampered treatment of a big leaguer. We didn't have iPads or iPhones available on our less-than-luxury busses; we didn't even have air-conditioning. But the ones we rode were the only ones we had in the '50s, so we were fine. In Nebraska we took the aptly named Jack Rabbit bus line. There were jackrabbits running to and fro across the roads wherever we went. It was hard to tell how many we hit, but it sure seemed like a lot. We occupied our time reading comic books, sports magazines, or just in general conversation with our teammates about their lives in the towns where they were raised. Occasionally, we just looked out the window at the cattle ranches and daydreamed about pitching to Mantle in The Show. That day was closer to reality than I thought it would be when I signed professionally just a few weeks before. The battle for the best seats on our trips to Kearney, Grand Island, Hastings, McCook, North Platte, Lexington, or Holdrege was dictated by which seat would be in the shade. Holdrege had by far the biggest mosquitos I had ever seen.

Our bus in Missoula was nicknamed the Iron Lung because of its shape. It had eight bunk beds, and we split time with teammates sleeping in on our overnight trips. Missoula to Boise, Idaho, is listed as about 367 driving miles or about an eight-hour trip. But with stops and the curvy, two-lane mountain roads, it was quite a trek in 1958. We would usually meet at The Turf Café in Missoula after we went home to pack our duffels for the upcoming trip, grab a bite to eat, and leave about midnight. After a few gas and diner stops along the way, we'd be in Boise a little after noon. Then we'd grab a short nap at our hotel and head to the ballpark. We didn't want to miss a chance to pitch to the future Mr. Baseball. Bob Uecker was Boise's cleanup hitter! Most of us were 19; Ueck was 24, a grizzled old veteran.

Many of our rides through Montana and Idaho were breathtaking, especially the snow-capped mountains and rock formations. We would occasionally have to stop because of a rockslide. There were no cell phones, but highway crews usually patrolled the roads. I wish I had pictures of us playing catch along the side of the road while waiting for them to clear the rocks off the roads.

The trip to Billings, Montana, could be a bit stressful for Chuck, our bus driver, travel coordinator, and trainer. As our trainer Chuck always had a towel and a can of ethyl chloride spray to numb the pain wherever we were hurting. And, of course, McKeon had a huge jug of his magic potion for sore arms: wintergreen oil, probably pickle brine, and maybe a little tobacco juice. It always seemed to be just the remedy for a sore or tired arm.

We had to go through a couple of mountain passes on the way to and from Billings, and in April they could be a bit slippery. Most of us were aware of the bus accident in 1946 that killed nine and injured six members of the Spokane Indians traveling through Snoqualmie Pass in rainy conditions. Most of the players on the Spokane team had recently returned from serving in the military during World War II. In 1959 when I was a member of the Class Double A Chattanooga Lookouts, we actually took some trips by train. And the busses were a step up from the Iron Lung of 1958.

The big story of 1959 was the gambling scandal in the Southern Association. There was always a section of guys seated in one section of Engel Stadium in Chattanooga, Tennessee. My roomie was Ernie Oravetz, a 5'4" switch-hitting outfielder and our leadoff man. I always wondered why some guys would ask Oravetz as we walked in the ballpark if he was going to take the first pitch or try to foul it off. These guys were way ahead of DraftKings. Eventually, George Trautman, the minor league commissioner, ordered an investigation, and two of our players got lifetime bans, and one or two received short suspensions. Jesse Levan, the ringleader, spent a little time in the majors with the Senators in 1954 and 1955. For a reputed $500, his career was over.

I was quite shocked when our manager John "Red" Marion (brother of Marty "Slats" Marion) called me in to his office in late July of 1959 to tell me that I was being called up to the majors to pitch against the White Sox the following Sunday at Comiskey Park in Chicago. I had a shoulder issue that had really compromised my pitching motion, but I didn't tell him that. I had struck out 19 against the Nashville Volunteers a few weeks before, setting a Southern Association record. After striking out the first four in my next start, my shoulder began to ache. Who knew why? There were no MRIs or X-rays back then. It was all by feel. Sandy Sandelin, our trainer, suggested I take 10 days off and rest it. It gave me a chance to go home to Zeeland to visit my parents and buy my first car: a used 1954 green Plymouth coupe, which cost $350. I wish I still had it.

My parents and an aunt and uncle had arrived in Chattanooga on Thursday to see me pitch the day I got called up. I was scheduled to pitch in the majors Sunday. When I returned from the 10-day layoff, my pitching motion was still not right. But Red Marion said, "tell them about it when you get up there."

Well, after watching me pitch the first couple of innings of my major league debut on August 2, 1959, Walter "Boom Boom" Beck, the Senators' pitching coach, could tell something was different. I only lasted a few innings. A week later I had a minor procedure to remove a fatty cyst from between my ribs on the left side of my back. The procedure did not leave much scar tissue.

In September of 1959, we stayed at the Kenmore Hotel in Boston, which was minutes from Fenway Park, where we were going to finish the season with a three-game series against the Boston Red Sox. I had seen the overhead view of Fenway in my dad's books titled *Who's Who in Baseball*, which he bought every year. I couldn't wait to walk over and see it from the inside. Security wasn't an issue at the time. I found an open gate. It was about 10:00 AM. Our game was scheduled for 1:00 PM. I had read that Ted Williams played pepper almost every day with Red Sox owner Tom Yawkey and clubhouse attendant Johnny Orlando. I found a seat in the front row between home and third and watched the great one tap balls to Yawkey and Orlando as they tossed them from about 25 feet. Pepper was a staple for big leaguers in those days. It was great exercise for hand-eye coordination. No one better at it than Williams. Then there was batting practice against some amateur pitchers they brought in to pitch. I was mesmerized, thinking about how I was about 50 feet from Williams. He was gangly, loud, and loved to swing a bat.

I didn't start that day. I got in in the seventh and pitched a perfect inning. Big deal. The Senators' brass wanted to see what my motion looked like after having the cyst removed. We lost 10–4, and our record fell to a major league worst 63–89. We lost again on Saturday, and then on September 27, the last day of the season, they decided to throw four of us new kids at the Sox. I didn't know I was starting until I got to the park. Our pitching coach had put a new baseball in my shoe. It was to be me for two innings, then Tom McAvoy, then Jack Kralick, and finally our $35,000 bonus baby, Lumenti.

I didn't last my two innings. I gave up six runs. Don Buddin, who wasn't known as a home-run hitter, hit a three-run shot off me, and Teddy Ballgame got two hits: a single and a double. I was done after one-and-a-third innings, in which I gave up five hits, a walk, and six runs. What a debut in Fenway Park! (Thank goodness I had some really good games there over the next 16 years.) After giving up singles to the first two batters, I turned around, looked at our second baseman Johnny Schaive, and mouthed: "I'm facing Ted Williams!"

That was a moment I'll never forget. I was fortunate to get to know Williams personally and spoke at the dedication of the Ted Williams Tunnel at the Boston Park Plaza Hotel on December 15, 1995, with many dignitaries like Curt Gowdy, Doris Kearns Goodwin, Larry Doby, Brooks Robinson, Ken Burns, *Good Morning America* host David Hartman, and future broadcast partner Bob Costas.

The 1959 season was over for me, but there were plenty of more significant events for me in 1959. I had met a girl, Julie Moore, that summer. I fell in love. Or at least I *thought* I did. We were married on October 3, 1959, in Chattanooga—the first of many mistakes I made away from the field. It took me 16 years to shed the guilt and make a break. I'll never forget my dad's words when I had to tell my parents I was getting a divorce. He said, "What took you so long?"

Parents didn't interfere with decisions their kids made in those days. You made decisions on your own and suffered the consequences if they were bad ones. Young men and women were pressured to get married and raise kids in those days. If you didn't get married when you were young, people would begin to question your sexual identity. I have two children, Jim

Jr. and Jill, from that marriage. That is the best part of that. They have produced five wonderful grandchildren. My veteran teammates in Chattanooga begged me not to get married. But the more they warned me, the more stubborn I got and the more determined I was to prove that I was right, and they were wrong.

In November of 1959, I saw my friend and teammate McAvoy do something twice that very few people see once. He broke his pitching arm throwing a ball. There have been a few pitchers who have done it, and most or all seem to be lefties. Mac was pitching for the Chattanooga Lookouts on a Sunday morning because of the extreme afternoon heat. After delivering a pitch, he let out a violent scream and rolled on the ground toward third base. He had broken the distal humerus. He was beginning to throw side sessions at Griffith Stadium, the home of the Senators, the following summer when his arm appeared to be healed. He was throwing so lightly. I was standing right behind him watching. Our trainer, Doc Lentz, asked him if he felt like he could throw a little harder. A few pitches into that and—*POP*—you could hear it. His broke his arm again. Mac's career was over. An arm injury is unpredictable, and those of us who have not had one that ends our careers are very fortunate.

The last part of the 1950s was quite an experience for me. Fidel Castro had taken over Cuba in 1959, so playing winter baseball there was out of the question. Too bad because that had been the most attractive place to play. After making $6,000 a year in the majors, you made $900 *a month* in Cuba, were provided an apartment on the boardwalk in Havana, played four days a week, and did not have to travel. So many great Cuban players have made it to the big leagues. I played with many of them because the Senators had a scout in Cuba known as "Papa" Joe Cambria. The Major League Baseball Players' Association had not yet been formed, and many of these Cuban players were happy to play for $4,000 or $5,000 a season. Our two best pitchers on the Senators were Camilo Pascual and Pedro Ramos. My teammate Zoilo Versalles won the American League MVP Award in 1965. Tony Oliva, a teammate and a good friend to this day, is the only player to win a batting title in his first two seasons; he did it in 1964 and 1965. Leading the league in batting meant something in those days.

So because there was no winter baseball in Cuba, organizations looked elsewhere. I went to Managua, Nicaragua, to pitch for the Bóer Indios, "the team of the people." Our manager was former big league first baseman Earl Torgeson. Each team was limited to four or five Americans. Former Red Sox shortstop Johnny Pesky managed Cinco Estrellas. Pesky and his wife became friends with my wife and me as we stayed in The Gran Hotel.

The Cinco Estrellas had a power hitter named Pedro Almendares. We only had four teams in the league so we saw a lot of Almendares. He was killing us with his prodigious home runs. Torgy had a meeting and said, "Are we going to continue to let this guy swing away freely against us, or is somebody going to push him off the plate?"

I was the starter that day. After throwing all strikes and retiring the side in order in the first inning, I proceeded to plunk Almendares in the ribs when he led off the second inning. Pesky, who was coaching third, was furious. He started to charge me from the coaching box. Almendares actually went back to the bench and was taken out of the game. I really don't think I threw hard enough to do any physical damage, but Pesky went a few weeks without speaking to me. There were no more couples' dinners. Later when he was coaching for the Red Sox and I was pitching for the Twins, we talked often about those days. The plunking of Almendares was forgotten.

Our second baseman was named Maury Lerner. He was an intense, tightly wound young man, a different kind of cat. After an 0-for-4 day, you could just see he was going to explode, hit something, or throw something. Lerner was in the Braves' organization and hit .328 in the Pioneer league for Boise the year before I played there. When Lerner passed away in 2013, I read his obit in *The New York Times*. Only then did I find out he became a different kind of hit man. He was known as "pro" or "Reno" and served time for murder. I got along well with Lerner. We talked hitting, pitching, and baseball in general. I'm happy that I never annoyed him.

I thought my career might end before it got started on our flight to Miami. We flew on Lanica Airlines. There were four passengers including us and a load of cargo. The plane was a DC-6 four-engine propeller-driven plane. About halfway through the flight, flames started shooting out of one engine. I quickly alerted the one flight attendant we had, and she rushed up to the cockpit. The pilot shut down the engine, and we continued to fly on to Miami.

CHAPTER 2
The 1960s

The last year of the original Washington Senators was in 1960, and I signed with them and wore their uniform in 1959 and 1960. The American League expanded in 1961 and added two teams: the second Washington Senators team and the Los Angeles Angels. The original Washington Senators moved to Minnesota and became the Minnesota Twins. Understandably, that has been confusing for many fans. The expansion Senators moved to Texas in 1972 and became the Texas Rangers. The nation's capital, Washington, D.C., was without a major league team in the country's No. 1 sport for 33 years until 2005 when the Expos moved from Montreal and became the Washington Nationals in the National League.

The year 1960 was chock full of highs and lows for me. My first highlight was making the Opening Day roster as the Senators took on the Boston Red Sox on April 18. That was very special then as there were only 16 teams in Major League Baseball—eight in each league. Oh, how I wish it was still that way. I can imagine the quality of baseball we would get to watch if that were the case. There were 16 teams each with a 25-man roster, only 400 major leaguers in the entire country—and I was grateful to be one of them.

Outgoing president Dwight D. Eisenhower threw out the ceremonial first pitch from his box seat at Griffith Stadium. Most of the Senators, including me, were gathered in a circle near the first-base line. Ike heaved a ball in the air, and we had a giant scrum to see who would catch it. Our bullpen coach, Clyde McCullough, a World War II veteran, captured it.

As we walked to the bullpen in in right-center field, we noticed how the flag was blowing straight in from center field. It was so stiff it looked like it was starched. We commented on how difficult it would be to hit a home run that day. Not for "Teddy Ballgame" aka Ted Williams. In the second inning, Williams drove a Camilo Pascual pitch 420 feet to straightaway center for a home run. It was the only run the Red Sox scored as Pascual struck out 15 in a complete-game, 10–1 win. That strikeout total is still an Opening Day record. Jim Lemon, Bob Allison, newly-acquired catcher Earl Battey, and even light-hitting Billy Consolo all homered for us. I say *us* because I was now a member of a major league team on Opening Day for the first time in my career. I would have the privilege of wearing a big league uniform on Opening Day for the next 24 seasons. What an honor!

Let's fast forward for a minute to 2006. I attended my friend and former teammate Bruce Sutter's induction ceremony in Cooperstown, New York. Sutter had me stand up for a moment and said, "I never played with a player who took more pride in wearing a big league uniform than Jim Kaat." I got a lump in my throat and swallowed hard. That was as touching a statement as anyone could make about my love and respect for the game.

My first legitimate start as part of a big league rotation came on April 22 against Boston. I had them shut out through seven innings until Frank Malzone, the high-ball-hitting third baseman for the Sox, took advantage of a letter-high fastball with a man on and tied the game. I was pinch hit for in the eighth, and we lost in 11 on a Vic Wertz home run. One consolation: I retired Teddy Ballgame on a fly out to left field in the eighth inning. I never forget a moment like that.

My one and only shining moment in the big leagues that season came on April 27 in Yankee Stadium. I was starting against the New York Yankees and their ace pitcher Whitey Ford. Whitey and I became friends 20 years later when I pitched for the Yankees, and we met in spring training. We continued that friendship through golf for many decades after that.

In those days the starting pitchers warmed up next to home plate and threw toward the backstop. This gave the fans a chance to see the pitchers up close. I could almost reach over and touch that No. 16 on Whitey's back as he warmed up on the Yankees' side of home plate. A pitcher spends a little time pitching from the stretch position, which he will do with men on base. As I went into my stretch position, I was looking right into the Yankees dugout, and Mickey Mantle, Yogi Berra, Bill "Moose" Skowron, Roger Maris, and Elston Howard were watching me. I opted not to look at them.

I did okay that day. I pitched seven innings and gave up one earned run on Skowron's home run. They scored three unearned runs in the fourth as second baseman Billy Gardner made a rare error. Whitey was cruising along after my buddy, Don Mincher, homered off him in the third inning. After we scored a run, Jim Lemon pinch hit for me in the eighth and hit a three-run homer off Whitey to make it 5–4. Pedro Ramos came in and shut the Yankees down the last two innings. I had recorded my first major league win. I was floating on cloud nine.

But I would come down from that cloud rather quickly. I found out I wasn't ready to pitch in the big leagues on a regular basis yet. I went 1–5 that season with an ERA of 5.58. I walked more batters than I struck out. Senators manager Cookie Lavagetto had called me in in May and said, "You'll be pitching every four days, so just relax."

He soon found out he couldn't honor that promise, and I didn't blame him. My Triple A manager Del Wilber had told me, "It's one thing to get to the majors, but it's another thing to actually *stay* there." I was optioned to our Triple A affiliate, the Charleston Senators in West Virginia, for a couple of months and then was called up in September and stayed on a big league roster for the next 24 seasons.

The offseason was an interesting one as I was invited to pitch in the Instructional League in St Petersburg, Florida. That was a developmental league that organizations sent their promising players to in hopes of speeding their rise to the majors. On November 26, 1960, came the news that the Senators were moving to Minnesota and would become the Twins. We were still playing in the Instructional League as the Senators, making for a weird situation. As players, we sat around and talked about what a good move this was for us. The Braves had moved from Boston to Milwaukee in 1953, and it had a positive effect on them. They went to the World Series twice—in 1957 and 1958. They won it in '57.

There was talk about how the players all got automobiles for the season for making appearances at local car dealers. When your salary was less than $7,000 a year, that was a big deal. We all saw it as a positive move, and it was. We were an improving team, and being in front of new fans would help us shed the label of being in Washington and known as "first in war, first in peace, last in the American league."

Speaking of cars, I did not want to spend hours driving to and from Metropolitan Stadium in Bloomington—not

far from the Minneapolis-St. Paul International Airport—
the Twins' new home. The park, which seated just more
than 30,000 fans, had been the home of the Minneapolis
Millers in the American Association. When I was with the
Charleston Senators in 1960, I had actually pitched a game
at Metropolitan Stadium against the Millers, the Red Sox's
Triple A team, featuring a 20-year-old Carl Yastrzemski.
So I found a home in the Minnehaha section of South
Minneapolis, a suburban area only about 15 minutes from the
stadium. A couple that had a summer lake home there made
their city home available for me to rent. For a few years in the
mid '60s, I worked as an ambassador for Cloverleaf Creamery
as one of my offseason jobs. I did a couple TV commercials
for them and autograph signings at supermarkets. They were
good people to work for and I enjoyed it.

When the Twins played the Yankees in Bloomington
in 1960, I asked Mickey Rendone, our visiting clubhouse
manager, if he could arrange an introduction for me with
Bobby Shantz, who was then with New York. This was a big
moment for me. I got to tell Shantz that he was my boyhood
idol and that I patterned my pitching motion (especially the
way I finished) after his.

I really felt I belonged in the big leagues the next year
because of the coaching of Eddie Lopat. It was like an
apprenticeship for me. Lopat was a 5'10" New York City

native who relied on guile, changing speeds on his curveball, and good control. Lopat taught me so much about how to pitch. My 9–17 record was not impressive, but I logged 200 innings, eight complete games, and gained the confidence necessary to believe that I belonged in a big league starting rotation. I threw my first shutout, and there was a game late in the year when I had a 6–0 lead and gave up back-to-back home runs in the seventh inning, but I came right back and finished a 6–2 complete-game win. Lopat said to me after the game, "Kid, you've arrived, you're maturing, you're trusting your stuff." Nice words to hear when your record was 5–12 after that game.

We were playing the White Sox in Chicago on June 19, 1962. Dom Zanni was on the mound for Chicago when I came to bat in the top of the fourth with the Twins up 4–0 with one out and the bases empty. I used our first baseman Don Mincher's bat. It was a Bobby Doerr model. Hillerich and Bradsby, which made bats under the brand name Louisville Slugger, had an initial and a number on the bat to identify which player had ordered that model. This one said "D112." I believe Ted Williams' bat said "W212," Ralph Kiner used a "K55" model, and Frank Robinson an "R161." "Minch" or "Mule," as we often called him, said, "If you're ahead in the count 2–0 or 3–1 or, of course, 3–2, expect a fastball." On a 3–2 count, I got a fastball from Zanni and drove it over the

375-foot marker in right-center. What a sweet feeling it is when that ball hits the sweet spot on the barrel of the bat. It's like hitting a golf shot flush in the sweet spot of the golf club. That happens maybe twice a round for me in golf.

My record in 1962 was just 10–9, but I got a letter from Ralph Houk, the manager for the Yankees and the American League All-Star team, that I had been selected to be on the American League team. Two All-Star Games were played from 1959 to 1962. The second game was included to increase television revenue for the players' pension fund and to boost income for Major League Baseball's operating offices. I didn't pitch in the '62 All-Star Game, but it was quite a thrill being there and looking at the stars that I knew from my trading cards. It was mind-boggling that I was on the same team as Berra, Luis Aparicio, Maris, Al Kaline, and Brooks Robinson.

In the winter of 1962, I was living in St. Petersburg, Florida. I settled in there for a few winters because I played in the Instructional League there and picked up a job working for the St. Petersburg Recreation Department in the offseason. I coached boys basketball and refereed games for them. I also played softball and basketball in an independent league with Don Zimmer and Hal Lanier. When I got my copy of *The Sporting News*, I saw an article about the Rawlings Gold Glove Awards. I had never heard of them until I read that article. And lo and behold, there was my picture as the winner of that award for American League pitchers, which was voted on by coaches and managers. So I mailed a letter to my dad to tell him about the award.

Nowadays, Rawlings stages quite an annual event at The Plaza Hotel in New York City to announce and honor the current winners. I am honored to be a presenter for the award to the pitchers in each league, and occasionally they have me present a legacy award to a former pitcher. I presented Whitey Ford with that award. A couple of years ago, I had a once-in-a-lifetime honor. Mike Thompson of Rawlings contacted me and asked if I had ever heard of Bobby Shantz. I told him he was my boyhood idol. Thompson said, "We would like you to present a legacy award to Bobby at the dinner this year."

So in front of hundreds of people at the event, I said "How often does an 80 year old get to present an award to his boyhood idol, who is 93?" I cited all his statistics from 1952 when he won the American League MVP Award. Johnny Bench was even shocked when he found out about that. It actually had some people in tears. Shantz and I had great visits during those two days. He is now 95, and I stay in touch with him.

I often wondered if the reason they awarded me the Gold Glove in 1962 was because of an incident that happened on July 24 that year. In the seventh inning, I took a one-hopper, which skidded off the bat of the Detroit Tigers' Bubba

Morton, in the teeth. Tigers pitcher Jim Bunning was one of the first players to run to the mound. The ball bounced to Rich Rollins at third base and became an infield single. I was stunned for an instant. Vic Power came to the mound, and as I was laying there, he said in his broken English, "You want to keep this for a souvenir?" I still have the ball with my teeth marks in it. It had the tooth fragments for a while.

This happened on a Tuesday night. My next start was to be the following Saturday afternoon in Cleveland against the Indians. Our owner, Calvin Griffith, did not like to put players on the disabled list because he would have to continue to pay them and he would also have to pay whoever replaced them. However, the Twins did want to replace me. But I resisted. I insisted that the Twins get me a rubber mouthpiece like boxers wore and allow me to make my next start. I did, and Willie Tasby and Willie Kirkland made the first two outs for the Indians on sharp ground balls back to me. I was cured from fearing a line drive might hit me. I pitched a complete nine-inning game that day, and we won 5–2.

There was one positive to my injury. Pitchers always ran sprints every day. It was supposed to build up our legs. We now know that's not accurate. I told Gordon Maltzberger, our pitching coach, that it was difficult for me to run sprints because every stride I took jarred my jaw, and I had several stitches in my mouth. So I was excused from running sprints.

Maltzy said, "You're probably going to tire in the latter innings because your legs won't be strong."

Well, this is very self-serving, but if you check our game log after my incident on July 24, I pitched nine innings in Cleveland and got a W and then 11 innings in Baltimore four days later. That was one of my most memorable wins because of the duel with future Hall of Famer Robin Roberts. I got the winning RBI in the 11th. Then I went 10 innings for a win against the Tigers before enduring a tough 1–0 loss to Dean Chance and the Angels in 11 innings. So much for not running causing me to lose leg strength!

That year was my breakout year in the majors. It's when I felt like I belonged. I went 18–14 with a 3.14 ERA, 16 complete games, and five shutouts. If you notice records of starters in that era, we suffered more losses than starters who are pitching in the specialization era, where multiple relievers are used to save games. We were usually left in until we gave up the lead. It was our game to win or lose. Our contracts were dependent on wins, not ERAs or keeping our team in the game. We had had 27 saves as a team that year spread among eight different pitchers. I even had a save that year. Our starting staff had 53 complete games and figured in about 130 decisions.

Despite a mediocre season in 1963 and a 10–10 record, I had one great moment. We played an exhibition game against the Milwaukee Braves at Metropolitan Stadium in Bloomington. I asked one of our coaches, Ed Fitz Gerald, if he knew Warren Spahn. Through 1962 Spahn had already won 327 games and was on his way to a National League record of 363 wins (which still stands) and a plaque in the Baseball Hall of Fame. He said he did and proceeded to track him down and introduce me. Spahn invited me to go to our bullpen and he watched me throw for a while. Then Spahn made a few suggestions. Spahnie was a toe-to-toe pitcher. His motion was less rotational and more linear and vertical like the face of a clock when it is 6:00. If you saw Sandy Koufax's motion or Ron Guidry's, those are similar to Spahnie's. So as an experiment, I started rocking to and fro from toe to toe and bending my torso toward home plate. He believed the pitching motion was torso and head toward the ground like you're bending over to pick something up off the ground. That felt pretty natural to me. As we left for our respective sides of the field, he stopped and said, "Kid, one more thing. When the game is tied in the seventh inning, it's just starting. You have to pitch a lot of hitters differently in the fourth at-bat than you did in the first three at-bats."

Point taken. I then asked him if I could have one more question: "How did you condition your arm in spring training?" He told me how he went to shallow center field with a leather bag of balls. (All ball bags were real leather in those days.) He then made a hop, step, and throw motion and threw the ball into second base on one hop. He then increased the distance a little every other day. In the spring of 1964, I did that. Coaches and veterans were beside themselves saying, "What are you doing? That can't be good for your arm!"

I asked them, "Any of you ever hear of Warren Spahn?"

After my first start following Spahn's lesson, I went nine innings, struck out 11, issued just one walk, and hit a three-run homer. We won 5–0. That was my last win and complete game of 1963. We did well as a team that year despite my mediocrity. We were getting better every year and had the Yankees in our sights.

There was a big difference between the amount of fame that came with being associated with the Yankees—opposed to the Twins. My Twins teammates and I weren't very recognizable or requested for many personal appearances because Major League Baseball was new to the Twin Cities. I compare that to the mid '90s when I began to do games on the Yankees cable network, MSG. After a half a season and with the Yankees having a successful year, our TV ratings were high. I would be walking down Park, Lexington, or 5th Avenue, and bus drivers, cabbies, and pedestrians would stop me and actually refer to specific things I had said in the previous night's game that they enjoyed. Wow—a country boy from Michigan getting that kind of recognition in the middle of Manhattan!

But back in 1964, the Twins finished four games under .500 after finishing 20 and 21 games over the two previous seasons. Horse trainers call that the "bounce theory." A horse is on the rise and suddenly runs a bad race. The horse bounces back. I was fortunate to bounce forward from my disappointing 1963 season, but the big story in 1964 was the emergence of a young player from Cuba. Tony Oliva defected in 1961, coming up through Central America and Mexico. His story is legendary. He arrived for spring training late in 1961 so the Twins released him initially. He was not a good outfielder, and the front office didn't get much chance to see him swing the bat.

The Godfather of the young Cuban players was Cristobal "Minnie" Mendoza, a stabilizing figure for them and—except for 16 games in The Show—a minor league lifer. He had the biggest smile on the planet. Oliva trailed him to Charlotte, North Carolina, the Twins' Single A affiliate, and took batting practice with his fellow Cubans. Phil Howser, the Charlotte general manager and a relative of the Twins' Calvin Griffith, contacted Griffith (who was both the the Twins' owner and general manager) and said that maybe they should sign the young Oliva and send him to Wytheville, Virginia, in the Appalachian League. They did. He hit .410 for Wytheville in

1961. The Twins brought him up and he made his big league debut on September 9, 1962.

In 1964, his first full season, Oliva led the American League, batting .323 and was named Rookie of the Year. He led it the next year too, hitting .321. He's still the only player to be batting champion in his first two big league seasons. He also led the league in batting in 1971 (.337). Oh, and by the way, after playing in the Instructional League and working on his fielding, he became a Gold Glove outfielder in 1966.

I remember the time we spent together in the Instructional League in St. Petersburg, where Wilber would hit him fly ball after fly ball until he could catch them routinely. I was the halfway person on those days, throwing the balls back to Wilber so he could keep hitting them. Oliva remains a great friend. He was a wonderful teammate and was elected to the Twins Hall of Fame in 2000.

In the early years of the Twins, we would get asked what the "TC" on our caps meant. Not many outside of the upper Midwest knew that Minneapolis and St. Paul were known as the Twin Cities. So we would say, "Twenty Cubans!" That got their attention. The Washington Senators had a Cuban scout named "Papa" Joe Cambria. He recruited the best Cuban players to play Major League Baseball for the Senators. There was no Major League Players' Association then, and Calvin Griffith was signing these players for very little money. The

Cuban players on the Senators/Twins were good. Pascual was the ace of the Senators/Twins for years. Other good Cuban players were Ramos, Carlos Paula, Julio Becquer, José Valdivielso (later a Spanish radio broadcaster in New York), Sandy Valdespino (my roomie in Missoula, Montana), Zoilo Versalles, and Bert Cueto.

But 1965 was *the* year. We finally got the pitching and defense to match up with our powerful lineup and won the American League pennant. On April 12, 1965, I was scheduled to be the Opening Day starting pitcher for the Twins against the Yankees at Metropolitan Stadium. This was to be my first Opening Day start. But it had rained torrentially that morning, and as I tried to drive to the ballpark, the highway was flooded, and traffic was at a standstill. The traffic jam was so bad that many cars had been stopped. I was afraid that if I just waited for traffic to clear, I wouldn't make it to the ballpark on time. I had to make a phone call, but this was many years before cell phones. So I managed to turn my car around and drove back to my apartment in Burnsville to call my friend and former teammate, Paul Giel, who was then the sports director for WCCO radio. He arranged for the station's traffic helicopter to pick us up in the parking lot of the high school in Burnsville. There were four of us: Dick Stigman, Rich Rollins, Bill Bethea, and me.

A few minutes later, the WCCO traffic helicopter picked the four of us up and took us to the Metropolitan Stadium parking lot. Despite the weather and the traffic, the game went on. Art López of the Yankees, and Twins teammates Valdespino, and César Tovar, who became my very close friends, made their big league debuts for the Twins in that game. Umpire Jim Odom made his major league debut at third base. Jim Bouton started for New York. I singled off Bouton in the fifth, driving in Killebrew, to put the Twins up 4–0.

I had a 4–3 lead with two outs in the bottom of the ninth inning. López pinch ran for Mantle, who had singled and was on second base. Joe Pepitone hit a pop fly to Tovar, who was playing third base. I was on my way to shake hands with our catcher Jerry Zimmerman when Tovar, nicknamed "Pepe," just dropped the ball on his very first day in the big leagues. He felt terrible. We became close friends that day. Why? I went over to him on the bench and told him "Forget about it. Go knock in the winning run!" In the 11th inning, he did just that. It was a memorable Opening Day, but only 15,388 fans showed up for the game because of the flooding. But that game was a portent of things to come. The Twins went on to be the American League champions.

We won 102 games, seven games ahead of the Chicago White Sox and 25 ahead of the Yankees. My roommate that year was veteran reliever Johnny Klippstein. He was a member of the Los Angeles Dodgers when they won in 1959. About six weeks into the 1965 season, he said out of the blue, "We can win the pennant with this team!" Not bad for the once lowly Washington Senators!

We began to win series after series and were building up a lead. Klipper went 9–3 that year and saved five games. If you talk to fans of that team and those of us who were on the team, the signature game was the come-from-behind, 6–5 win against the Yankees on July 11. I started that game and got knocked around. I pitched four-and-one-third innings and gave up three runs. We were down 5–4 in the bottom of the ninth. Rich Rollins walked. Oliva flied out to center field. Then Harmon Killebrew must have fouled off five or six pitches (we didn't count them in those days) and then connected on a low fastball and homered to left field to give us the win. (The phrase "walk-off home run" wasn't used at the time.) That gave us a win in the four-game series instead of a split. It was the last game before the All-Star break. We were able to exhale and played quite stress-free in the second half to maintain our lead.

My personal thrill that season was pitching the pennant clincher on September 26. We beat the Senators in Washington 2–1, and I ended the game with a strikeout of a man in the bottom of the ninth who would eventually become one of my best friends in baseball: Zimmer.

We were on to the World Series to play the Dodgers with Koufax and Don Drysdale. Dick Weincek, the scout who had signed me, had scouted the Dodgers. He had pages of information about them, which he offered to share with me. This was years before interleague play, so, of course, we had never faced the Dodgers. I told Weincek not to be offended, but my thinking was that they had never faced me either or seen me pitch. I would let them try to figure me out.

Koufax opted not to pitch Game One because of his Jewish faith. It was Yom Kippur, the Jewish day of atonement. So Drysdale started Game One. We knocked him out early, and when manager Walter Alston went to the mound to remove him, Drysdale had a great line which I've used at award banquets and just in conversations with friends. Big D said to Alston: "I bet you wish *I* was Jewish!"

Then in Game Two, we got our first look at Koufax. I had never met him or seen him pitch. (No interleague games at the time.) I consider him a friend now and have such respect for him. He was the best pitcher of my playing days. Why? He pitched for a team that didn't score a lot of runs. It was customary at the time for the starting pitchers to pose for an Associated Press wire photo before the game. I could smell the hot liniment he had on his left arm to kill the elbow pain he was experiencing. It made my eyes water.

As we warmed up in the bullpens behind the fence in right-center field at Metropolitan Stadium in Bloomington before a crowd of 48,700, I could instantly see and hear what a live arm he had. The ball exploded out of his hand and made a loud sound when it hit the catcher's mitt. We were each perfect for the first three innings with the exception of one walked batter each. I sat next to Johnny Sain, our pitching coach, and whispered in his ear, "John, if I give up a run, this game is over!" Koufax was that impressive.

With the aid of a rare error by Jim "Junior" Gilliam in the sixth, we got a man on second. Then a double by Oliva and a single by Killer gave us a 2–0 lead. *I better make that stand up*, I said to myself. *We won't be getting any more.* I was very prescient. Not only didn't we score any more off Koufax in that game, but he shut us out in Game Five and then again in Game 7 by a 2–0 score on two-days' rest. In 24 innings he allowed one earned run.

But in Game Two, we got a little insurance against the Dodgers bullpen. I gave up a run in the seventh as the Dodgers bunched a few singles together, but I escaped with no further damage. I was in a little trouble in the fifth inning, but Allison, though not known as a superior outfielder, made one of the great catches in World Series history. If it happened today, it would be played over and over on highlight shows. With a runner on first, second baseman Jim Lefebvre hit a sinking line drive down the left-field line. Allison dove and half slid on the damp outfield grass. It had rained earlier in the day. He made the backhand catch, kept the runner at first, and I escaped. That catch was the play of the game.

An incident in our half of the eighth inning became a light-hearted moment a few years later. We had added one run off reliever Ron Perranoski in the seventh inning and were threatening again in the eighth. With runners on first and second, Frank Quilici batting, and me on deck, Perranoski balked *on purpose*. Then, as the runners advanced, first base was open. He walked Quilici intentionally because he had struck me out in the seventh and thought I would be easier to get out than Quilici. But I singled up the middle to give us a 5–1 lead, and that's how it ended. What a thrill—a complete-game World Series win against the Dodgers and Koufax! The 1965 Series is the last one in which every win was a complete-game victory by the starting pitchers. When Perranoski and I became teammates on the Twins from 1968 to 1970, he told me the story of the intentional balk in the 1965 Fall Classic. We later became golfing partners. Sadly, Perranoski passed away at age 84 on October 2, 2020.

We had a reunion of our 1965 American League pennant-winning Twins team in 2005. I would guess it is just in the last 10 to 15 years that they honor players or teams with big celebrations. When Herb Carneal, our longtime radio voice, and I were inducted into the Twins Hall of Fame in 2001, we each had about two minutes to make our acceptance remarks. There was no ceremony in 2020 because of Covid-19, but the previous two years when Johan Santana and Joe Nathan were inducted, they had 30 to 40 family members seated on the field and many former teammates. Michael Cuddyer presented the official blazer to Santana. Also present were all of us who were members of the Twins Hall of Fame with a nice video of their highlights. I'm not bitter about that. It's just a sign of the increased marketing and attention that these things seem to merit. I returned for the 50th reunion of our World Series team in 2015 and threw out the ceremonial first pitch. Torii Hunter caught it. I threw it from the rubber, right over the plate.

In 1966 the Twins shared a charter flight with the Yankees because of the airline machinists' strike, which lasted 43 days. It was big plane and typically usually used for international flights. The Yankees were on one side of the aisle, and the Twins were on the other side. We were going to Washington to play the new Senators, and the Yankees were going to play the Orioles in Baltimore, so they hitched a ride with us to Washington. We had played a day game and had to wait a while at the airport before the charter flight became available. The players had ample time in the airport lounge to have a few cocktails. Of course, many of the Yankees, like Mantle and Clete Boyer and others, were friends with Billy Martin, who was one of our coaches. Howard Fox, our traveling secretary, had his wife, Yvonne, a sweet woman who was classy in every way, on our flight. Between Martin and a few of the Yankees, it began to get a little noisy and profane. Fox asked Yankees Manager Houk if he could quiet things down. Houk, who had earned a Bronze Star and a Purple Heart during his service in the U.S. Army in World War II, still carried his military nickname of "The Major." Houk had a few strong words. When Houk spoke, things got quiet.

Later, when we got to our hotel in Washington and Fox was handing out our room keys, he slid Martin's across the check-in counter where it hit a wall and fell to the ground. As Martin bent over to pick it up, he sucker-punched Fox. It was ugly. That was strike one against Martin. Then, in 1969, a few of the team players and coaches were hanging out at the famous Lindell A.C., a popular bar for Detroit players. Alex Karras of the Detroit Lions received a suspension from NFL commissioner Pete Rozelle for gambling. Karras was a part owner of the Lindell A.C. Dave Boswell, one of our starting pitchers, and Art Fowler got in a dustup about something, and Martin walked over and asked Boswell to step outside. The real story of what happened next gets a bit fuzzy after that. I saw Boz the next morning, leaving his room as we were on the same floor at our hotel. He looked like he had been in a fight with Muhammad Ali. His eyes were swollen, and his face and cheeks were all bruised. I asked him what happened. He said Martin had a couple of his goons hold him, and Martin, well under the influence of some strong drinks, punched him over and over again.

Martin's story was that he hated to do it, but Boz started the fight and he had to defend himself. Boz was 6'3" and 185 pounds and a well-conditioned athlete. Martin was 5'11"and 160 and not in prime physical condition. Draw your own conclusions to who was telling the truth. That was strike two, and I think defying Griffith with some of his decisions that Griffith didn't like was strike three. Martin was fired after the 1969 season. He had a couple of off-field altercations, and Griffith had had enough of that kind of behavior.

Griffith and Fox, his confidant during my days there, made it very clear in their attitude toward all of us players, White or Black, that we were lucky to be able to play baseball. They were very condescending toward us. The only player he showed any affection for was Allison. I think he thought if he could be friends with Allison, who was the first Twins player to establish full-time residence in the Twin Cities, Allison could convince other players to do whatever Calvin suggested. That worked…for a while.

During one of my many contract negotiations, if you could call them that, he asked if I could "go out on Cedar Avenue [where Metropolitan Stadium was in Bloomington] and find a job that pays you what I'm offering you."

My hasty retort was: "Can you go out on Cedar Avenue and find a pitcher that will win 18 games for your team?"

This was years before free agency and arbitration. It was the greed of owners like Griffith and the lack of trust or any feeling of belonging to the organization that fostered the idea of free agency. Griffith and I would cross paths at the Metrodome. After he sold the team in 1984 and came to the games there, we ended up having a friendly relationship. The way he treated us and operated the team was standard operating procedure in the pre-free agency days. Not every owner operated like that, but certainly a majority did.

Before Griffith hired Martin, Cal Ermer took over as Twins manager in 1967 after Sam Mele was fired after 50 games, and we almost won the pennant. Ermer was accustomed to managing in the minors, disciplining players, and had different expectations for them. Now, he was dealing with players who were major league veterans and not accustomed to a lot of rules and regulations. In fact, the best managers I ever played for, Chuck Tanner and Whitey Herzog, had only two rules: show up on time and play hard every out.

We finished under .500 and in seventh place in the 10-team American League, 24 games behind the Tigers. So in 1969, Griffith hired Martin to manage the Twins. It was a popular choice. Martin had been a scout for the Twins, a coach on our 1965 team, a manager for the Twins' Triple A team, and was well-connected with the front office. As the slogan goes today, he checked a lot of boxes.

Things were different and things could get chaotic. In the dugout Martin was a genius. But away from the field, his behavior caused him a lot of problems. He had a hard time telling the truth to a player if it meant causing a confrontation. For example, my dad had a stroke in 1969. In those days a player couldn't just get family leave for a week. You barely got one day. I pitched on a Saturday in Cleveland and wouldn't be due to pitch again until Thursday of the following week. We had an off day on Monday but were playing an exhibition game in Milwaukee. I was the Twins' player representative at the time. I asked Martin if I could go home from Cleveland to visit my dad. I'd meet the team at home on Tuesday. He said yes. It was raining in Milwaukee, and they wanted to talk to the player reps about the possibilities of playing or not playing. Griffith, the team's owner and general manager, was there and came into the clubhouse to seek me out. I was at my parents' home in Michigan. Griffith asked Martin where

I was, and Martin said he didn't know. "I guess he missed the flight," he said.

Griffith was understandably angry and called me into his office on Tuesday. He was calling other teams in an attempt to trade me. He didn't like what he thought was my insubordination. When I told him the story, he softened. He said, "I'm finding out that Billy has lied to me about a few things this season."

Martin had so many great skills for running a game. Just like his personality, he was feisty, aggressive, fearless, and tempestuous. I saw him from every possible viewpoint. The Twins traded for Martin as a player on June 1, 1961. A week late, he was in the lineup when I started against the Orioles. I was 1–5, just cutting my teeth on being a regular starter, and as you can see by my record, I wasn't doing very well. Neither was our team. We had lost 13 straight games. I singled in the top of the third, and Martin homered to give us a 2–0 lead. In the eighth inning, I singled again and scored on a sacrifice fly. We won 3–1 and broke our 13-game losing streak. Martin and I were the stars of that game and we had our picture taken for the Minnesota papers after the game. He was a big deal, a former Yankees World Series hero. I called my dad the next day to tell him that my photograph with Martin was in the paper and that we won 3–1. I was excited. I was now 2–5.

Martin became friends with some of the Griffith family—Twins farm director Sherry Robertson, Billy Robertson, and Joe Haynes—who were executives with the Twins. After the Twins released Martin, he became a scout for the Twins and in 1965 and was added to their coaching staff. Griffith had retained Early Wynn as our pitching coach from the 1968 staff. Wynn was a Hall of Fame pitcher, but as a coach he didn't offer much other than hollering at the pitchers, "Hey, meat, get your running in now." "Meat" was short for "meathead," which veterans often called younger players. Wynn liked his booze, and if he had a rough night before our next game, he was ornery. Martin wanted Art Fowler, who had pitched in the majors for nine years and had been Martin's pitching coach in Denver. Fowler was also Martin's drinking buddy. In those years it was customary for managers to pick their buddies for coaches—not for their coaching skills, but as their confidants and off-the-field companionship.

So Martin called me and invited me to have lunch with him at Howard Wong's, which was a popular postgame spot for Martin. He told me that Griffith wanted Wynn as his pitching coach but that he wanted Fowler for the job. Martin said, "I know you don't care to run like most pitchers; you get your leg work shagging flies and fielding ground balls." Fowler was not a fan of pitchers running. He liked to see his pitchers throw more. Out of 25 pitches, he could dot the knee-high outside corner with 20 of them. His battle cry was "Babe Ruth's dead! Throw the effing ball over the plate."

Another one of his favorites when he was questioned about not running the pitchers was, "Jesse Owens never won no games. You can't run the ball over the plate." We loved Fowler. What a circus as they both were on the staff! Wynn would chase us down and tell us to get our running in, and we would go near Fowler and say, "Artie, take us down to the bullpen and show us how to throw strikes," just to get away from Wynn. Starters loved Martin because he would live and die with them. He gave us a long leash. I pitched 242 innings that year in just 32 starts. That's an average of more than seven innings per start.

That theory started with my first start of the year. I thought I had strained a muscle in my upper thigh on my left leg diving for a line drive, which Lou Brock hit in my last start in spring training. I deflected it and dove to pick it up. I knew I had pulled or strained or torn something. I later found out that I had torn a muscle, but I finished the inning. Then I was scheduled to start the second game of the season, which was coming up in Kansas City in five days. Martin noticed me limping and asked if I thought I could pitch. I said that I'd like to try. So I started the second game of the season. Fowler would check with me every few innings to ask if it was okay. I learned years ago that you don't give a manager a reason to take you out. You let *him* make that decision. After 11 innings I came out with the game tied at three. That was the enjoyable thing about pitching for Martin.

The thing that made pitching for Martin tough was his second-guessing. He hated to see a hitter get a hit on a fastball. If he had his way, he would have pitchers throw all curves. A lot of managers are like that because when they were players, they couldn't hit a curve so they thought we should throw a curve *on every pitch*. It got to be a joke between pitchers and catchers when we gave up a hit on a fastball, and he would scream at the catcher. We would tell him after the inning that it was a breaking ball that didn't spin much, which was also known as a "hanger."

If Martin thought you didn't throw the pitch he wished you had thrown, he'd have Fowler approach you the next day or two. Fowler would whisper in his thick South Carolina accent, "Billy thought you should have thrown a curve to Pagliaroni in Seattle the other night."

I had started a game on a Thursday night and gone only five-and-one-third innings before getting a lucky win. So then on Saturday in Seattle, I did my usual pregame throwing before the game. We got involved in an extra-inning game that night, and Martin asked me if I thought I could pitch an inning. I entered the game as a pinch-hitter in the top of the 14th inning and walked. I stayed in the game and pitched the bottom of the 14th inning. We scored a run in the 15th inning. I stayed in and with one out gave up a home run to Jim Pagliaroni on a lengthy at-bat. I threw him curves, fastballs, more curves, then more fastballs. On what must have been the 10th pitch of the at-bat, he homered on a fastball, which I didn't get in on his hands. I pitched the 16th inning, and the game was called because of a Sunday curfew law in Seattle. The game was tied at seven. We won the game the next day in the 18th inning.

The interesting thing about that was as that the start was delayed, we looked up at the Moon and the public-address announcer said, "Man has just landed on the Moon." I remember looking up at the Moon on our flight back to Minnesota and marveling at the fact that way up there in the sky a man had landed on the Moon, and we were 30,000 feet in the air.

After Fowler delivered Martin's message to me, I went straight for Martin's door and asked if I could have a word with him. Behind closed doors, I said, "Billy, if you want to call my pitches *before* I throw them, go ahead and do it. But don't send Artie to deliver your second-guessing *after* I have thrown a pitch."

He sat in complete silence and after a while said, "I shouldn't have done that." He couldn't help himself. It was just his impulsive nature.

We clinched the American League West in the first year of divisional play with nine games remaining in the season. So it was time to prepare for the playoffs against the Baltimore Orioles, the winners of the American League East who finished 19 games ahead of the Tigers. Martin went upstairs to meet with Griffith and ask who he thought should be the starters in the playoffs. Jim Perry and Boswell were the logical choices, having each won 20 games. They were easily our two best starters. I had not pitched well in September, finishing the season 14–13. Griffith said Perry, Boswell, and Kaat. Martin said, "I'm going to start Bob Miller in Game Three." He may have thought that because the Orioles had a lot of very good right-handed batters or because I wasn't pitching well that "Foot" was the better choice. (We called Miller "Foot" because his foot clicked every step he took due to an ankle injury he had suffered years ago.)

We got swept by the Orioles. They were really good. Their starters were Cy Young-caliber. They had power, great defense, and a deep bullpen. Hey, they won 109 games in the AL East, a much stronger division than the West. The first two games of the first American League Championship Series still rank as two of the best from my viewpoint. Perry and Mike Cuellar both pitched great baseball. We took a 3–2 lead to the bottom of the ninth. I was a spectator and a cheerleader that entire series. I sat in the bullpen in case I got the call to pitch.

Perranoski, our closer, was warming up because John "Boog" Powell, a power-hitting lefty, was the O's leadoff batter. We were shocked that Martin didn't bring Perranoski in to face him, but Martin stuck with his starters if they were pitching well, and Perry had been pitching *very* well. Leading off the bottom of the ninth inning, Boog homered to tie the game at three. We lost in the 12th on Paul Blair's bunt single with Mark Belanger on third.

In Game Two, Boswell and Dave McNally dueled to a 0–0 tie, heading into the bottom of the 11th inning when the O's parlayed a walk, a sacrifice bunt, and an opposite-field single into a 1–0 win. They won two extra-inning, one-run games with great starting pitching, great defense, and fundamental baseball. They blew us out in Game Three, and Martin only stayed with "Foot" for an inning and two-thirds. I saw no action in that series.

Martin wasn't the only one who caused skirmishes. In July of 1967, we were playing the Kansas City Athletics. Killebrew was on second base, and Oliva singled. Kansas City catcher Phil Roof blocked the plate and forced Killebrew to slide around him, but Killebrew never reached the plate. Our dugout erupted because they thought Roof's play was illegal or dirty. Jim "Mudcat" Grant argued so vehemently that home-plate umpire John Stevens ejected him. An inning later Roof came to bat, and because of the sentiment on our team,

I hit him in the ribs with a pitch. Then their dugout erupted. Nothing came of it, but Roof glared at me and trotted down to first base.

Four year later, the Twins acquired Roof in a trade. When he walked through the clubhouse door, we looked at each other. I walked over to him and said, "We're on the same team now." He chuckled, and all was forgotten. A few months later, our manager Bill Rigney put him in the lineup on a day I was pitching. We shut out the Angels 1–0 for a complete-game shutout. Roof caught me twice more before the end of the season. Both games we synced up like magic. One of them was another shutout. I told Rigney the next year that if it was possible—without causing any disharmony—that I would like Roof to catch me. I didn't dislike George Mitterand at all. Mitterand and I had some good games together, but you'd have to be a pitcher to understand the connection between a pitcher and a catcher. That's why they call it a battery.

So in 1972 "Rig" started putting Roof in the lineup for my starts. On July 2 I slid into second base to break up a double play and felt a sting in my lift wrist. I pitched two-and-a-third innings after that, but my left hand was so swollen I had to come out of the game. We won that game, and it ran my record to 10–2. With an ERA of 2.06 and five complete games, I was leading or co-leading the league in most pitching categories with future friend and Hall of Famer Jim Palmer.

As I looked back at that years later, I think I should have put up more of a fight to try to pitch my next start just to see how it reacted. After all, I did pitch two-and-a-third innings after the slide. Why couldn't I pitch more? Unfortunately, I didn't fight it as Dr. Harvey O'Phelan, our orthopedic surgeon, said that if I continued to pitch, my wrist might not heal properly. I respected him and his opinions very much. My season was over. Instead of heading to the All-Star Game, I was headed to a three-month vacation. Teams had no rehab programs in those days. You just rested until it healed.

In the last two games of the 1967 season, the Twins needed to win just one to be the American League champions. Ermer took over for Mele 50 games into the season. My record was 1–8. When I pitched poorly, I got plenty of run support. When I pitched well, there was not much run support. That's a bad combination. But things began to turn around for me, and by September 1, I was 9–13, which was still not a good record. I, though, found a little magic between my August 26 start, where I gave up five runs in five innings, and my next start on September 1 was a complete-game win. I gave up two earned runs and surprisingly I was striking out more batters than usual. My arm suddenly had some life to it, and my breaking stuff was crisper. And then it started: a seven-game roll such as I had never experienced. My line from September of 1967: seven games started, six complete games, 65⅔ innings pitches, 55 hits allowed, 11 earned runs, six walks, 65 strikeouts, a record of 7–0, and an ERA of 1.55, though I probably pitched too many innings. I averaged nine innings per start. I was now 16–13. And now I was about to start the most important game of my career on September 30 against the Red Sox.

Four teams were in contention to win the American League pennant in September. The White Sox dropped out earlier that week when the A's swept them a doubleheader. There were just two games left in the season, and if I won, we would be American League champs and I would be starting against the St. Louis Cardinals and Bob Gibson in the World Series the following week. The Cardinals had already clinched the National League pennant. I spent a lot of time laying on the training table and chatting with Koufax, who had retired after the 1966 season and was on hand to be one of the announcers on ABC. That was a good way to pass the time because that hour before going out to warm up was the most nervous time for a starting pitcher.

The day game was played before a packed house of 32,909 at Fenway Park. The game started out fine for us. We could have had a big first inning. The bases were loaded with one run in already and Rod Carew at the plate. Carew hit a line drive to Rico Petrocelli for out No. 2, and Ted Uhlaender grounded out. We led 1–0. The first two-and-a-third innings went well for me. I even struck out Reggie Smith, who pretty much owned me. And then while throwing a pitch to José Santiago, the pitcher, in the bottom of the third inning, I felt like I had hit my funny bone on a table. It was my humerus. A couple more pitches floated up to home plate like I was lobbing the ball to the catcher. It was obvious I had suffered a game-ending injury and had to come out. The injury was the injury that now requires the famous Tommy John surgery. But Dr. Frank Jobe did not invent that career-saving procedure (ulnar collateral ligament reconstruction) until 1974.

Killebrew homered in the top of the ninth to narrow Boston's lead to just 6–4, but it was not enough. We eventually lost that game by that score. My future friend and teammate-to-be, Jim Lonborg, threw a gem the next day, and we were headed home. That was the most disappointing moment of my career. The Tigers still had a chance to tie the Red Sox on the last day of the season, but they lost Game Two of a doubleheader to the Angels and what was to become a saying for Red Sox fans for years (and still is) was born: "The Impossible Dream." I am flattered when Red Sox fans and even Yaz and Hawk Harrelson tell me if I hadn't injured my arm, they may not have won.

Speaking of medical operations, I watched pioneering surgeons Dr. Denton Cooley and Dr. Michael Debakey perform open-heart surgery from an observation dome at the

Texas Heart Institute in Houston in the late 1960s. I became cognizant of my need for a healthy diet and I was motivated to try to avoid heart disease. So I stopped eating red meat for a while. It has worked. I am 83 as I write this and I play a round of golf almost every day.

In 1969 I was getting my left thigh injected with Novocain before every start because of the groin injury I incurred in spring training. I had no feeling in that leg. I was okay to push off the rubber on a pitch, but when I had to field a bunt or a ball, I had to brace my left leg and lost balance. Luckily, I didn't make more errors. I was very surprised that I was awarded the Gold Glove that season. (Ironically, before a game, in which I made three errors, I was presented the Gold Glove for 1968.) After the season the area had calcified, and I had surgery to shave it off. Unfortunately, at the time there were no muscle-sparing or arthroscopic procedures. They just cut through muscle until they fixed the problem. I don't think my left leg ever got back to the strength it had before the injury.

That season was one of our most interesting ones. We had a very good team. Carew stole home seven times—a testament to Martin's aggressive style of play. He also hit .332 and won the American League batting title. Killebrew hit 49 home runs and won Most Valuable Player of the American League. Oliva led the league with 197 hits. Perry and Boswell each won 20 games—numbers worthy of a championship team—but the Orioles played just a shade better in the American League Championship Series and went on to the World Series. The sad thing about the 1969 season: it wasn't a season of joy like the one I experienced with the 1982 Cardinals. There was too much chaos. Martin was a lightning rod, as trouble found him and he found it so easily.

CHAPTER 3

The 1970s

The 1970s was the most active decade of my playing career. By the end of the decade, I had played for four different major league teams. My Washington Senators/Minnesota Twins days were over. I was claimed off waivers by the Chicago White Sox on August 15, 1973 after the Twins thought my career was over. I had another 14-win season and I was gradually coming back from my 1967 elbow surgery, but that was still not enough to avoid a pay cut. My annual salary had dropped to under $50,000—down from my high of $60,000 in 1968. I had a decent year: 14 wins, 10 losses, an ERA in the mid 3.00s, a few complete games, and a couple of shutouts. But I had the 25-win season in 1966 before the injury and 14-win seasons in 1968, '69, and '70. If I had gone 14, 14, 14, 16, 25, I would have continued to get raises each year, but because the 25-win season came when I was 27 years old, each season was judged by that. According to our owner and general manager Calvin Griffith, I had nowhere to go without free agency or arbitration. Suck it up and pitch, which I did in 1971.

My won-loss record, however, was 13–14 (my first losing record since 1961), and they paid pitchers solely for getting wins. My 260-plus innings, 3.32 ERA, 15 complete games, including four shutouts were of less significance to them. I was back to my pre-injury form, but my record didn't show that. Griffith cared about wins, not team records. The Twins were 74–86 and finished in fifth place in the American League West, 26½ games behind the Oakland A's. Today the writers, who vote for the Cy Young Award, are beginning to measure pitching effectiveness by something other than wins: ERA, base runners per nine innings pitched, strikeout/walk ratio, run support, and innings pitched. Griffith said, "With a record under .500, I have to cut you."

I had taken up golf a couple years earlier and I said: "Let's play golf for it." He wouldn't bite. To my mind, 1971 was very close to 1966 in terms of my effectiveness. Wins and losses don't always tell the full story of how effectively one has pitched. Fast forward a few decades to 2010 when "King" Félix Hernández of the Seattle Mariners won a Cy Young Award in the American League despite not winning 20 games. He was 13–12. More recently, Jacob deGrom of the New York Mets won the National League Cy Young Award in 2018 when his record was just 10–9 and again in 2019 with a record of 11–8.

After the 1971 season, Marvin Miller, who became the executive director of the Major League Players Association in 1966, and Jim Bunning, the Philadelphia Phillies' players' representative and later the National League players' representative, suggested I try to play a season without signing a contract. If you didn't sign by a particular date in late March, a team could retain you for a year by just renewing your contract from the previous season, even though you didn't sign it. They suggested Joe Torre do the same as Torre had contract issues with Paul Richards of the Atlanta Braves. The attempt after the 1969 season by Curt Flood to challenge the reserve clause scared me off. It cost Flood the rest of his career. He sued and took his case to the Supreme Court of the United States. Unfortunately, he lost. With a wife and two children, that would have been quite a risk for me, a risk I didn't dare take.

Here is another example of Griffith's miserly ways. After the 1971 season, my neighbor in St. Petersburg, Florida, Don Zimmer, who played in Japan, suggested I contacted Tak Ishikawa of the Hankyu Braves club. They were interested in acquiring a left-handed pitcher. Griffith had told me I had very little value now. Ishikawa would have signed me to a two-year contract for $125,000 per year if he didn't have to pay too much to Griffith to purchase my contract. I thought he could purchase it for $50,000 tops. Unfortunately, Griffith asked for $150,000 for my contract. There went my chances of pitching in Japan and maybe getting a chance to pitch to Sadaharu Oh, the Japanese home run champion with 868.

Bunning had a big influence in the dealings of the Major League Players Association. He and Miller both thought it was ridiculous that I was forced to take a pay cut for four consecutive seasons, considering the record I had during those years. Sometimes I wish I had followed their advice. I'm just happy that arbitrator Peter Seitz ruled in 1976 in favor of players being free to move about, and the players today are benefitting from that. I don't feel sorry at all for ownership because of what I went through with Griffith. They could have met us halfway in finding some way for us to not be tied forever to one team who refused to pay us our worth. The owners' arrogance and unreasonable tactics have caused the tail to wag the dog. The players and agents now swing a lot more weight than when I played.

In the early 1970s, Marv Grissom, a right-handed pitcher, was now our pitching coach. Grissom threw a screwball during his playing days. Very few righties threw a screwball. Some lefties, like Carl Hubbell, Warren Spahn, and Fernando Valenzuela, had one because years ago there were fewer left-handed batters, so lefties wanted a pitch that broke down and away from right-handed batters. Why? Most right-handed batters, particularly power hitters, wanted to pull the ball. The screwball, which breaks the opposite of a curveball, was a good pitch to get righties to hit off the end of the bat. From a lefty pitcher, the curve breaks down and in. A screwball or "scroogie," as it was often called, breaks down and away. Probably the most famous lefty who possessed a great "scroogie" was Hubbell. From 1928 to 1943, he won 253 games—all for the New York Giants—had five 20-win seasons, and is a Hall of Famer. In more recent decades, lefties like Frank Viola, Tom Glavine, John Franco, Johan Santana, and Jamie Moyer developed excellent change-ups that had the same effect as a "scroogie" without all the wrist action. The wrist action on a screwball is that the hand turns inward with the palm facing outward to impart the screwball spin. They did it with the way they held the ball.

Since I didn't have as much bite anymore on my short or quick curve (nowadays it would be called a slider), I decided to go with a fastball, curveball, and screwball. If you want to have a long career as a pitcher in the big leagues, you have to keep adjusting and trying to improve—unless you're Nolan Ryan, Sandy Koufax, or another elite pitcher. I was not one of those. I didn't get batters out. I tried to give them opportunities to get *themselves* out with movement, changes of speed, and good control. My new mix was working beautifully until July 1. My record was 10–2 with an ERA just over 2.00 and five complete games. I even hit a couple of home runs and was batting .289 in the last year pitchers would bat in the

American League. The designated hitter rule went into effect in 1973. I enjoyed batting and still despise the designated hitter rule, the playoffs, the nit-picky rules in effect now, the specialization of pitchers. The game is no longer. Baseball is specialized powerball.

But if the designated hitter rule had gone into effect earlier, I could've avoided a major injury. On July 1, 1972 in the top of the sixth inning, I slid into second base and jammed my left wrist. Of course, there were no sliding gloves then. I broke the navicular bone in my left wrist. I pitched two-and-two-thirds innings after that, but my hand had swollen to the point where I couldn't grip the ball and was done for the season. In retrospect, I have often thought that since I pitched more than two innings with a broken wrist, what if I had just iced it down? Could I have made my next start? If an injury like that happened today, they'd treat it, but I've been told that you can't operate on a fractured navicular bone.

I had a normal offseason of resting my arm and letting my wrist heal. I played a lot of racquetball—frequently with Minnesota Vikings coaches Bud Grant, Buster Mertes, and Jerry Burns and my friend Mahlon Greenberg, a local attorney. Grant was as steely and competitive on the court as he was on the sideline. I usually went home with a lot of red welts on my back because he would try to intimidate me into moving out of his way. I could be as stubborn as Grant.

After I saw and read about guys missing starts because of injuries, I made a commitment to myself: unless my arm was broken, I wanted to pitch. I figured I might have 10 to 15 years to do this if I was good enough. I didn't want to miss any opportunities because of a minor injury. Unfortunately, I did have a couple of major ones, including that torn elbow ligament before Tommy John surgery existed and that broken wrist sliding into second base in 1972. But if I was physically able to pitch, I pitched.

I was very curious about what my 1973 contract might look like. Like every other player in the majors at the time, my contracts were one-year contracts. The terms "multi-year" and "long-term," as applied to baseball contracts, did not exist. Would Griffith look at it from a viewpoint of me on my way to having one of the best years of my career? Or would he say, "I can't help it if you injured your wrist; you only won 10 games?" I already knew the answer to that question.

January was the month we began checking our mail and wondering what our contract would say. When my contract arrived, I saw that it called for the same amount of money I had been paid in 1972—$46,000. I was not happy. I met with Griffith and told him that I would not sign a contract for 1973 for less than $60,000. I was prepared to sit out the year if necessary. My family and I had moved to Apopka, Florida, just north of Orlando. To stay in shape, I was working out with the Rollins College baseball team, pitching plenty of batting practice and running fielding drills with the team. Griffith eventually sent his son, Clark, to present me with a new offer. I took it out of the envelope and read it. The offer was not even close to the $60,000 I was determined to get before I signed. I said, "Clarkie, you're wasting your time and gas money. I am not signing for less than $60,000." Clark still lives in the Twin Cities and texts me about baseball from time to time. I consider him a friend.

Spring training was almost over, I still hadn't signed, and the Twins were getting ready to leave for Oakland to open the season. I don't remember pitching in any exhibition games. I don't think I was allowed to do that without a signed contract. But I told Frank Quilici, the Twins' manager, that I would be ready to pitch if I signed a contract before Opening Day. Howard Fox, the team traveling secretary who later became the team president, called me. Fox and I were not close friends. Obviously, we knew each other well from the 16 years I had been in the organization, but to me and the other players, he was "ownership." I didn't know what the owner/player relationship was on other teams, but on the Senators/Twins, there was a huge divide between them. No social activity. No casual conversations. Only contract negotiations.

Fox said, "The boss has your contract ready."

So I went down to his suite in our hotel. Calvin Griffith was there too. He smoked cigarettes through a long gold cigarette holder. He was smoking as he stared out the window with his back to me. "Your contract is on the table." I checked it over; it was for $60,000. We had discussed a bonus for my 11 Gold Glove Awards (at that point) so I brought that up. I struck a nerve. "Sign the damn contract," he said, "or I'll take it off the table."

I slowly read it and signed it. I walked over to him to shake his hand and more or less said, "This is over. Let's move on." No hand was offered to shake. Fox didn't utter a word.

I returned to my room and said to my roommate, Phil Roof, "I got the $60,000, but I will assure you that I won't be with the Twins when the season is over. They have had enough of me." I had signed 15 one-year contracts with the Twins. I had led the team in most career pitching categories up to that point. It was always cool and flattering to see that I was second in so many statistical categories to the great Walter Johnson. That was heady stuff! But of the 15 contracts I was offered, seven called for salary cuts to begin negotiations. Another seven started with modest salary raises. And my 1973 contract started with the same salary as the year before.

I started the Twins' third game of the 1973 season. I felt fine. I pitched okay, going five-and-one-third innings with just one earned run to pick up the W. Lasting just more than five innings was not considered much of a start for a starting pitcher. We called them "five and fly." Some pitchers enjoyed coming out of a game after they had pitched five innings, just enough to qualify for the win. I actually got off to a pretty good start. My record was better than I deserved, but it caught up with me later.

On July 1 I probably pitched as well as I ever pitched in a game. It was against the California Angels. Frank Robinson led off the bottom of the second inning with a home run. Winston Llenas reached base on an error in the seventh. That was the only time I had to pitch out of the stretch. Rod Carew knocked in a pair in the top of the third inning, and we won 2–1. Bill Singer and I went the distance. I think that's the closest I ever came to a no-hitter or a perfect game. We played that game in one hour and 40 minutes. The significance of the time was quite humorous. It was fireworks night, and the game started at 6:00 PM. It ended at 7:40, but it was not yet dark enough in Anaheim, California, for the fireworks. So our bus left the "Big A" with the 27,068 fans still waiting to see the fireworks.

That moved my record to 9–6. I shut out the New York Yankees and Mel Stottlemyre four days later and then on July 22 earned—and I used the term loosely—my final win as a Twins pitcher. It was against my good-friend-to-be Bill Lee of the Boston Red Sox. The score was 10–7. I didn't pitch well. Then I started getting what I probably deserved. I gave up five runs, four runs, and then capped off my Twins' career on August 7 by giving up five runs in the first inning in my penultimate start. The Twins had seen enough. My prediction would be confirmed. The Twins placed me on waivers, thinking that, at 34, my career was over. My ERA was over 4.00, and my record was under .500. I couldn't blame them.

I had told Quilici, our manager and my former teammate and friend, that I did not want him to feel any sentimental obligation to keep starting me. Despite my ineffectiveness at the end, I had told Bob "Buck" Rodgers, our bullpen coach, that they were making a mistake. My arm felt good. I was gaining a little arm strength. I had lost the feel of my screwball after breaking my wrist the season before, but I just didn't execute my other pitches. I had poor control and I had given up 26 home runs in just over 180 innings. That's pathetic.

I was playing golf at the Minnetonka Country Club, where I was a member. I was getting ready to putt on the sixth green when one of our assistant professionals drove up to the green. "Mr. Kaat, there is a man named Roland Hemond on the phone for you."

Hemond had called my house and was told that I was out on the golf course. (This was, of course, before cell phones.) Hemond was the general manager of the White Sox and would become a good friend. Hemond proceeded to tell me that the White Sox had claimed me off the waiver list and informed me that I was the first player who was affected by the 10-and-5 rule: as a player with 10 years in the majors and the past five with the same team, I had the right to refuse the claim.

I was surprised that the White Sox claimed me. I had heard rumors that the Kansas City Royals or the Yankees might have an interest because they were in the pennant race. The White Sox were not. Hemond said that they were looking ahead to the next season, and Johnny Sain was their pitching coach. The White Sox felt I could still be an effective pitcher. At 34 I had already pitched about 2,500 innings, but I wasn't pitching well at the time. Hemond then proceeded to really excite me. He said, "Your contract now is for $60,000. We are prepared to sign you for 1974 right now for $70,000."

Are you kidding? Send me the contract and the pen over the phone! I'm all in, I thought. I would have to have back-to-back 20-win seasons to get Griffith to give me that kind of raise. The sad part of all this is that in my head I would have liked to have been a Twins pitcher for my entire career. I never heard from Griffith or Fox. I went in to thank Quilici. The Twins had a game to play shortly, so he didn't have a lot of time, but he told me, "I would like to have kept you, but Calvin doesn't think you can pitch anymore."

I reached Griffith by phone later that day to tell him that I had enjoyed my 16 years in the organization. His reply was priceless: "I was in favor of keeping you, but Quilici didn't think you could pitch anymore."

Clearly, someone wasn't telling the truth, but I was raised to do the right thing and I thought saying a civil good-bye was the right thing to do. Now, it was on to Chicago. As my family and I were leaving Minneapolis and driving out of the metro area, I got quite sentimental. I didn't want to leave, but it turned out the best for me and Dave Goltz, a Minnesota native, who took my spot in the rotation. He had enough success to sign a nice free-agent contract with the Los Angeles Dodgers a few years later.

My first big adjustment to playing for the White Sox was wearing the red shoes that their players wore. Chuck Tanner, the White Sox manager who was the epitome of the glass half-full person, told me that I would be starting on August 26 against the Detroit Tigers. It was always difficult for me to navigate through the Tigers' lineup. I spent the 10 days leading up to that working with Sain every day. We worked on spin. I tightened up my breaking ball with a little more relaxed grip with lightened thumb pressure. I pitched well on August 26 as we beat the Tigers 4–1. I went the distance, allowed just three hits with no walks. Frank Howard got two of his three hits off me. I, though, was off to a nice start with my new team. I went 4–1 the last six weeks of the season and got my record to 15–13. It was a time when players and many owners conducted business like they were enemies and not all members of the same team. Thankfully, things have changed.

After joining the White Sox, I immediately bonded with Dick Allen. He had come off an MVP year in 1972, when he almost singlehandedly willed the White Sox to winning the American League West. The A's ended up beating them out by five-and-a-half games. The White Sox attendance had dropped to under 500,000. In 1972, during Allen's MVP year, they drew more than 1.7 million, and the next two seasons well over one million. Allen led them out of the wilderness like Moses led the Israelites out of Egypt centuries ago. So we often called him "Mose," short for Moses.

In late June of 1973, Allen suffered a broken leg and didn't play the rest of that season. As soon as he found out I enjoyed watching thoroughbred horses run as well as baseball, we began to visit more and more. We lived in the same apartment complex on the west side in 1974. In the few years we were teammates in Chicago and Philadelphia, I saw him do legendary things on the field and talked baseball with him a lot. He learned how to play the game while mastering situational baseball under Gene Mauch in Philadelphia. If there was a man on second with no outs, at least hit a ground ball to the right side and advance the runner to third.

If there was a man on third and no more than one out, hit a ground ball to the right side with the infield playing back and drive in the runner from third. We called it "playing to the scoreboard." The score, the inning, and the count on the batter determined how you would pitch or hit.

That's why I probably remember so many stories about my years with Allen and had memorable moments with him. In 1974 I was pitching a game in Cleveland, and we were leading the Indians 4–0 in the bottom of the seventh inning. With the bases loaded and no outs, Dave Duncan grounded into a double play. Thinking there were *three* outs, Allen flipped the ball to the first-base umpire as was his custom after the third out. The umpire jumped out of the way to avoid the flip, and two runs scored. That made it 4–2. As we trotted off the field after the third out, Allen said to me, "I'm sorry 'Old Timer.' I'll get those two back for you." He then hit a two-run homer in the ninth, and we won by four. He started calling me "Old Timer" because of my years in the game, and at that time, I was the oldest player on the team.

One time before a game Don Unferth, our public-relations man, brought Elliott Gould to the dugout to meet Allen. While the opposing team took batting practice, Allen and I were often seated on the top of the dugout bench. We couldn't see the whole field from the bench as the dugout was obviously below field level. We were talking baseball. Allen wore his hard hat as he always did since the Philly fans threw batteries and other hard objects at him in his days there. As usual, Allen was smoking a heater. Allen was insecure and shied away from attention, and I think that's why he smoked. It was a nervous or bad habit like we all have somewhere in our lives. He was as friendly as could be to Gould. After Gould finished visiting, Allen said, "Old Timer, what's he do?"

I told him that he was a famous actor, appeared in *M*A*S*H*, and was married to Barbra Streisand. Allen asked, "Can he hit a curveball?" He laughed as only he could laugh. He was merely saying he was more impressed with a good hitter than a famous actor.

You will seldom, if ever, see a picture of Allen in a short-sleeve shirt. On an exceptionally hot day in 1974, I said, "Dick, it's a 100 degrees out. What's with the long wool shirt?"

"Don't want to show them the ammunition, Old Timer." He meant he didn't want to showcase his large, muscular arms, which looked like a blacksmith's.

This is a bit self-serving, but a great memory for me occurred in the summer of 1974. Ryan of the Angels was in the process of pitching another no-hitter against our White Sox team in Chicago. I gave up a solo home run to Robinson in the top of the second, and it still stood at 1–0 as we trotted off the field after the top of the ninth inning. Allen tapped me on the backside on the way to our third-base dugout and said, "Old Timer, we're going to win this one for you." After Jorge Orta struck out for Ryan's 13th K of the game, Allen hit what appeared to be a harmless two-hop, ground-out to third baseman Rudy Meoli, who did the standard hop, step, and throw to first, but Allen beat it by a half step. An error and two soft singles later, we had a 2–1 win. If Allen doesn't beat that ball out, I doubt we win that game. He was more than a power hitter. A former All-American high school basketball player at Wampum High in Pennsylvania, he was quite the athlete.

Another legendary thing he would do occasionally is "hit a hole in the wind." In the spring on a cold night, we sat in the dugout at Comiskey Park just prior to the start of the game with the wind blowing in. The players would look at the flagpole and see the wind direction and say, "*Nobody* is gonna hit one out of here tonight." Allen would look at me and wink and, sure enough, he'd hit a laser right through the wind into the bleachers.

Allen was serious about having everybody on his team play the game the right way. Many fans may not remember that Chicago Cubs legendary third baseman Ron Santo, a future Hall of Famer, actually finished his career on the south side with the White Sox. Santo was an emotional player, and the deep dimensions at Comiskey compared to the friendly confines of Wrigley Field were frustrating him as his fly balls at Comiskey probably would've been home runs in Wrigley. We had a runner on second and no outs in a game when Santo hit a fly ball to left-center for an easy out. When he returned to the dugout, he spun his helmet toward the helmet rack in disgust. As it spun, it nicked Allen's shoe. No harm done, but Allen looked at Santo and said, "What we needed was a ground ball to second, not a fly ball." The dugout got as quiet as a crowded elevator, but Santo was wise enough not to challenge Allen on that and quietly sat down. Point made.

A couple of my favorite times with Allen were in 1976 when we were teammates with the Phillies. Allen had actually encouraged the Phillies to acquire me when he heard they were considering getting a veteran pitcher in the offseason. On our first trip to Cincinnati, I told him on the flight that I would like to take him to see a special athlete while we were there. It meant he'd have to get up early one morning, but it would be worth it. I rented a car, and we drove to Paris—Paris, Kentucky, where perhaps the greatest racehorse of all time, Secretariat, was stabled. Seth Hancock, the managing partner of Claiborne Farm, had arranged for us to tour the farm and see "Big Red," as they called Secretariat. The hour-and-a-half drive to Paris and back to Cincinnati lent itself to memorable talk on our two favorite subjects: horses and baseball. I had mentioned several times to Allen that I'd like to see his farm in Perkasie, Pennsylvania, outside of Philadelphia. "Come out anytime, Old Timer," Allen would say.

He gave me the address, but we had no GPS in those days. So after the 1976 season, I asked Richie Ashburn, legendary Phillies announcer and a Hall of Fame player for the Phils, if he knew how to find Allen's farm. Fortunately, Ashburn had been there and wrote out the directions. You couldn't call Allen. He just wouldn't answer his phone. I found Allen's house and farm and knocked on the door. Cold and gray outside, it was Election Day in November. Allen barely opened a curtain and peeked out to see who was knocking. Next thing you know we're headed to the barn where he kept a very promising colt he owned named Briar Bend. His stall needed cleaning. Because of the weather, I wore jeans and a wool shirt. He had two pitchforks, and away we went. We must have "mucked out," meaning cleaned the stall, for more than an hour and talked baseball the whole time. The Phillies had won the division that year, and it was the first time Allen had a chance to play in postseason games. We had reason to celebrate. Because it was Election Day, no alcoholic beverages were served until 7:00 PM. "Old Timer, we need a little taste," he said, "after working like we did, cleaning out the stall." He knew a little cafe where the owner gave us two paper cups and poured us a small glass of wine, and we toasted the 1976

Phillies. That was the last real personal contact I had with Allen other than seeing each other briefly at a baseball event like a memorabilia show. Forty-five years later, the memories are as fresh as if they happened this past season. You never forget keeping company with a legend!

I staged a baseball camp in 1973 because I had met Jim Dimick, the coach at St. Olaf College, at a sports banquet in the Twin Cities. He was an outstanding man of good character. We ran it for two weeks in the summer using the college facilities. Giving pitching clinics to young boys is difficult because the baseball is too big for them to grip it the way an adult can. I could just talk to them about the mechanics of a pitching motion and how to bunt and run the bases properly. The highlight was having some youngsters from Quilici's neighborhood in Chicago as guests. As their chaperone drove them from Chicago to Northfield, Minnesota, the home of St. Olaf, they saw livestock, including cows and pigs. That was their big topic of conversation. They had never been out of the city and had never seen barn animals. We all got a good laugh out of hearing them describing that. It was a nice, relaxing offseason. I played lots of golf and I had a concrete block built in my backyard in Florida to do some throwing. This is something Sain used in the offseason. It was about 4' x 3' and framed in 2' x 4's. I angled it with the two struts attached to it. When the ball hit the block, it bounced back to me. I took a bag full of old baseballs with me after the season. It also helped me work on my fielding. I could spin the ball and make it glance off the block in different directions.

The 1974 season was quite an eye-opener. I started the year 4–1 but really wasn't pitching well enough to deserve to be 4–1. The game has a way of evening things out. I lost the next five decisions and went to 4–6. My last start was in Boston, where I gave up five runs in two-plus-innings to the Red Sox. When we returned home from that road trip, Tanner came over to me as we were awaiting our luggage at the airport. He said, "Could you come in a little early tomorrow? I'd like to talk to you one-on-one."

Of course, he was going to tell me that the Sox were going to release me. He would say how I had a nice 15-year career, yada, yada, yada. That's what I was prepared for. But Tanner said, "You've been winning 15 games a year for 15 years in this league. I think you can still do it. I'm going to start you a week from Monday in Cleveland on June 18. You and Sain go to the bullpen every day and try to work things out. I may even bring you in as a reliever."

I actually picked up a cheap win, coming in for a two-inning stint and giving up a run. I would say that any other manager, including Whitey Herzog, who was a great in-game manager, would have released me after July 2. But Sain and I figured out a few things, or I should say: Sain figured out a few things. Use a quicker release, gamble early in the count, and challenge batters to make contact. The thinking was: no nibbling or fear of contact. I told our veteran catcher Ed Herrmann to put the signs down quickly, set up in the middle of the plate, and signal for all fastballs. I'd wipe my right thigh with my glove if I wanted to switch to a breaking ball.

Sain was so helpful to my career. With his guidance I believe I was the first pitcher to use the slide step with a runner on first base. I developed it to combat the base-stealing proclivities of Bert Campaneris and Herb Washington. The latter was the Oakland Athletics' designated runner. I don't think Lou Brock of the St. Louis Cardinals, whom I had faced in spring training games and later in the National League, ever attempted to steal a base against me because he said he couldn't get a decent jump because of the slide step. I could occasionally deliver the ball to the plate in under one second. Most of the time, it took me 1.0 to 1.2 seconds. That was not enough time to steal.

Anyhow, on June 18 I went the distance against the Indians in Cleveland, walked just one, and we won 7–3. My future teammate and friend George Hendricks hit two home runs for Cleveland. Allen and Orta each hit two for our team. Four days later on June 22, our win was one of the top moments of enjoyment in my career. I was facing my former team, the Twins. Orta hit a two-run homer in the top of the

10th inning, and we won 3–1. I walked just one and went the distance. My former buddies, including Harmon Killebrew, Rod Carew, and Tony Oliva, who were responsible for many of my wins in my Twins' days, went a combined 1-for-12 against me. Carew got the one hit. When Glenn Borgmann grounded out for the final out, I let out a whoop and looked up at the Twins' owner's box and said, "Take *that*, Calvin!"

The fact that I walked just one batter was particularly important because I had been pitching too cautiously and falling behind. With Sain's suggestion of a quicker release and working at a quicker tempo, I had a 7–6 record. I rattled off a few consecutive wins, lost a few, won a few more, and on September 1, my record stood at 14–13. I got on a roll in September with four good starts and four wins. Meanwhile, Wilbur Wood, a teammate who was a knuckleball pitcher, was accustomed to starting anywhere from 44 to 49 games a season. Wood's record was now 20–19. He was 24–20 in 1973. Tanner didn't want him to lose 20 games again. Tanner came to me and said, "Any time you're ready, I'll start you." I started on September 22nd and won my 19th game.

Then in Texas to face the Rangers, we got rained out for two days after having an off day on the 23rd. So I started again on the 26th and pitched back-to-back games. I won my 20th game. I got to start again on the second-to-last game on October 1 and won my 21st game. I was so grateful to Tanner.

I went from thinking my career was over to going 17–7 the last three months to finish the season at 21–13. I owe both Tanner and Sain. In the offseason Hemond offered me a contract for $100,000. I wouldn't even think about asking him for any more. He had rescued me from the waiver list, and I proved that I could still pitch.

I had another enjoyable year in 1975. I got off to a great start: 5–0, then 8–1. By the All-Star break, I was 13–5. I lost a tough one in my last start before the break. Tom Walker outpitched me, and the Tigers won 2–1 in one hour and 38 minutes. That was one of the quickest games of the year. I was selected to be one of the pitchers on the American League All-Star team. This stuff was surreal after my struggles in Minnesota in my final season there. I pitched two scoreless innings in that All-Star Game in Milwaukee's County Stadium, retiring all six batters I faced. When facing Johnny Bench, I threw him a sloooow curve. (In 2020 Zack Greinke threw one, which was clocked in the low 60s.) Bench waited and waited and waited and then hit it way over the left-field wall but about 50 feet foul. He grinned at me and mouthed, "Throw it to me again!" I did. He waited a little longer, but he still flied out to left field.

My performance fell off in the second half of the 1975 season as I went 7–9. I can understand why pitchers might have to miss a start once in a while or get an extra day's rest.

After the great September of 1974 and the start of the 1975 season, my stuff was not alive in the second half, especially in September. I got my 20th win, and it came against the Twins on September 6, but I lost my last three games, including a tough 2–1 loss to my buddy Eddie Bane, the Twins' top draft choice in 1973. My record for 1975 was 20–14, but I think I should have finished stronger.

It was quite a reversal of fortune from 1974. White Sox broadcaster Harry Caray had been calling for my head: "I don't know why Tanner keeps running him out there. When your slow curve and your fastball are the same speed, it's time to call it a career!" In the last home series of the year, Caray was handing out his player awards. He approached me in our dugout and said, "Jimmy, I named you the White Sox Pitcher of the Year and I want to give you a television set on my pregame show."

I said, "Harry, stick your TV where the sun don't shine. I don't want your TV set. Give it to Terry Forster. He saved a lot of my wins." Off I walked.

The unique thing about Caray is that he announced a game like a fan. He was so critical of players over the air, but in my case, he never admitted he was wrong after my second half. Next spring at the team spring training hotel, however, he approached me and said, "Jimmy, sit down and let me buy you a drink." He wasn't trying to say he was wrong about me.

He was just being sociable. You couldn't insult, embarrass, or anger him. Caray never took it personally. It was just his job to announce like a fan. He would have players' wives in tears with some of his commentary.

After my 1975 season, Hemond told me I would be due for a nice raise. John Allyn, the White Sox' owner, however, was losing money every year. There were three teams in the National League East, which were looking for a veteran starting pitcher: the Mets, the Phillies, and the Pittsburgh Pirates. Roland asked me, "Where would your preference be if we worked out a trade? We think we could get a few young players for you."

I had been following the Phillies in spring training the past few years, and they were getting better every season. So I told him the Phillies. Lo and behold, I received a phone call in early December from Paul Owens, the Phillies' general manager. He was at the Winter Meetings. He said that the Phillies had just finalized a trade with the White Sox to acquire me. On December 10, 1975, the White Sox traded shortstop Mike Buskey and me to the Phillies in the National League for pitchers Dick Ruthven and Roy Thomas and utility player Alan Bannister.

Of course, I had never played in the National League. My previous 18 years with the Senators/Twins and White Sox were all in the American. I didn't notice an enormous difference, but there was indeed a difference: National League umpires used the inside chest protector, not the outside balloon that umpires in the American League used. (The AL switched to the inside chest protector for all new umpires in 1977. Established umpires were allowed to continue to use the old ones.) With the inside chest protectors, umpires got a better look at the ball as it crossed the plate and they called more low borderline pitches strikes. So I think that was a change for the better for me. Not only did I have to get used to the 12 stadiums in the National League, but I also had to familiarize myself with 350 batters. And when I batted, I had to be familiar with a league full of new pitchers.

My friend, statistician Peter Hirdt, compiled statistics for me years ago, comparing my numbers to other American League pitchers from 1961 to 1975 to point out that if had I retired after the 1975 season, I would've been inducted in the Hall of Fame much sooner. In those years I was first in wins (234), games started (509), innings pitched (3,580), second in complete games with 63 to Mickey Lolich, and third in strikeouts with 2,124 behind only Lolich and "Sudden" Sam McDowell. I have included these stats here not to boast but to point out how many of the members of the Veterans Committee do not do their homework.

Regardless, I was pleased to join the Phillies. "The Pope," as we called Owens because he looked like Pope Paul VI, gave me a nice raise to $150,000. The Phillies had the best team I ever played for from a physical talent and experience standpoint. However, Danny Ozark, who was a fine gentleman and a longtime Dodgers coach, was the Phillies' manager. He was the least skilled manager I ever played for in the big leagues. He was pleasant and not volatile or critical. But he just didn't seem to have a feel for the game like Tanner, Herzog, or Billy Martin did. Tanner spoke with Ozark and told him to pitch me as often as possible. I wasn't a power pitcher anymore, but I pitched 303 innings in 1975 and depended on a heavy workload to stay sharp with my control and rhythm.

There was a lockout in the spring of 1976 because the owners were not willing to admit that free agency had arrived. They wanted to appeal and fight it. They lost. They were arrogant and selfish and treated players like we had no rights except to play for them. Then it came back to bite them where it hurt.

I didn't know many of my new Phillies teammates, so it was an awkward spring. Bob Boone and Mike Schmidt began to contact players, and we gathered at a local college field and held informal workouts during the lockout. The issue was settled in two weeks, and we went to spring training in Clearwater, Florida, for real. As we got closer to Opening Day, I was announced as the Opening Day starter. That made no sense to me. Future Hall of Famer Steve Carlton, who had gone 27–10 for a club that won only 59 games, was bypassed. I asked for a meeting with Ozark to explain how awkward that was for me. I was the new guy on the team, not as decorated as Carlton, so why wouldn't he start Carlton? Ozark said he thought that having Carlton start Game Two would make him more relaxed. Hogwash. Ozark had a grudge against "Lefty," as we all came to call him, and this was his way of using it.

Fortunately, Lefty became one of my closest friends on the Phillies. They had a number of veterans on those teams in 1976, '77, and '78. Tim McCarver is one of my closest friends to this day. Allen and I became close friends the year before in Chicago with the White Sox. Schmidt, Garry Maddox, Jim Lonborg, Tommy Hutton, Davey Johnson, Boone, Johnny Oates, Tug McGraw, and I all became close.

I started the opener at home before 42,000 fans in Veterans Stadium on April 10 and did okay. I went seven innings and gave up only two earned runs. We scored three in the seventh to take a 4–3 lead against the Pirates, but they tied it in the ninth and won it 5–4 in the 11th. Two starts later on April 20, I got my first National League win against the Pirates at Three Rivers Stadium in Pittsburgh, a 5–1 complete game played in one hour and 47 minutes. The position players loved it.

Then things hit a snag. I had a few rough starts and an occasional good one, but Ozark insisted on skipping me against teams that were loaded with right-handed batters. I mentioned slyly to him that up to that point I had pitched about 3,500 innings in the majors. That's 10,000 outs. A majority of those were right-handed batters. I actually went to Owens and suggested that he try to move me to another ballclub. The way Ozark was using me, they were not going to get the best out of me. I used to kid him and say, "Danny, Walter Johnson died years ago. You're stuck with us mortals."

But that trade was not going to happen. Phillies' management was convinced that Ozark was a good baseball man because he had been in the Dodgers' organization for 20-some years. He *was* a good baseball man, but he was in over his head managing. There was rampant talk on the team that we would win in spite of him. Some remarked that he was like a grandfather to us, but not a leader.

On July 11, 1976 before 46,807 fans packed into Veterans Stadium, I pitched a complete-game 3–0 shutout of the San Diego Padres in 96 minutes. I hit a single in the seventh inning. The most damaging blow came on August 8. I had run off a number of good starts and got to 10–4. Then I lost a 3–2 game to the Mets on July 30 and a couple other close ones. I had pitched on August 7 against the Cardinals in St. Louis, dressed in my rubber nub shoes in the dugout in the eighth.

Those shoes were not conducive to running. The Cardinals had a promotional event prior to that game so there was no pregame practice. I usually played catch and fielded a few ground balls the day after I pitched, but that was not possible on the field that day. With the game tied at two in the ninth inning and one out, Greg Luzinski singled. Suddenly, Ozark looked at me and said, "Go run for Bull." *Really? No pregame warmup? No spikes? I hadn't been called on to pinch run in years.* Not wanting to cause a confrontation, I jogged to first base, hoping that Jay Johnstone would hit the first pitch out of the park and I could trot around the bases. Instead my worst nightmare happened. Johnstone drove a double into the gap. I came chugging around second and because of the loose dirt in the infield I had no traction. I half slid, half stumbled into third, banging my right knee pretty hard in the process. Oates had to come in and run for me! Oatsey scored, and we won the game 3–2.

My season or time in Philly would never be the same. My knee was swollen so badly I could barely get my trousers over my knee. Ozark saw me limping and said, "What happened?"

I said, "Danny, I should have told you I couldn't run. You never used me like that before. I wasn't loose. I had no spikes on." He burped and shrugged and said, "Oh."

I started a few times, and my record went to 12–14 by the end of the season. I was both angry and sick to my stomach over the incident. I loved being part of this team, but now I was of no use to them. I wasn't capable of performing because of my knee. The treatment I got was something fairly new called cryotherapy. A long cuff was wrapped around my right leg, and then ice cold water flowed through the channels attached to the cuff.

I started and got my last win on September 27. I asked Ozark the next day if he had plans for me to pitch in the upcoming National League Championship Series. He said no. He was planning to go with Carlton and Lonborg in the first and second games, which was understandable. And then he'd go with Larry Christianson or Tommy Underwood, who were both young and inexperienced. No problem. I just wanted to know so I could prepare myself with my throwing program. I usually threw a little bit every day anyway.

In those days the National League Championship Series was a best-of-five series. We had five days off before the first game. The Cincinnati Reds thumped us pretty badly in the first two games in Philadelphia. So when, on our flight to Cincinnati, Ozark asked me whether I could start Game Three, I emphatically told him yes. He said he didn't want to start either of the "kids" in that situation since we were down two games on the road. I never wanted to miss a start. The following day would mark two weeks since my last start. Fortunately, the next day was an off day, and we had a workout.

I spent a lot of time fielding ground balls at shortstop with Larry Bowa, our starting shortstop, and throwing to first base. That was one of my favorite drills. I learned from Spahn back in 1963 that is the most natural way to throw a ball.

In Game Three I had the Reds shut out on two hits through six innings. We scored two in the seventh to go up 3–0. Then Ken Griffey Sr. chopped one off the turf for an infield hit, and Joe Morgan walked on a few pitches that would have been strikes were we not in Cincinnati in front of the home crowd of over 55,000. I glared at home-plate umpire Dick Stello. He turned away; he knew the hometown rules. Out came Ozark. They hadn't hit a ball hard yet. He burped and said, "I'm bringing in Reed."

Ron Reed was a terrific reliever who had a good fastball. I said, "Danny, these guys are fastball hitters. I'm doing okay with my soft stuff and control."

I didn't win that argument. A couple of hits, a walk, and a triple by César Gerónimo, and the inning ended with the Reds up 4–3. But the Fightin' Phils fought back and took a 6–4 lead going into the bottom of the ninth inning. Reed was still pitching. To lead off the bottom of the ninth inning, George Foster and Bench hit back-to-back home runs off Reed to tie the game. A few batters later, Griffey hit an infield single off Underwood with the bases loaded. Dave Concepcion scored, and the Reds won 7–6. It was a tough spot for a young, inexperienced pitcher—or even a veteran. I felt bad for Underwood. The Phillies won 101 games that year. In fact, they won at least 100 games in each of my three years in Philadelphia. They were one of the best teams I played on, but we couldn't get through the NLCS.

The next season was the most disappointing year of my career, as far as pitching performance was concerned. Randy Lerch, a lefty with Carlton-like potential, was probably going to be a starter, and the Phillies, like most teams, began to use a five-man rotation. Wayne Twitchell was a hard-throwing righty with promise. I really had to have an effective spring training performance to be a part of the rotation. Between my knee injury in late 1976 and an arm that had no life in it anymore, I had to dazzle them with something. I was like a rookie trying to earn a spot on the staff. I understood that.

So I was penciled in to face the Reds and I knew that how I pitched could determine my spot on the staff. I was pleased that McCarver was the starting catcher that day. He was as savvy a catcher as there was calling a game. Of course, he caught all of Carlton's starts. The Reds brought a lot of their regulars to play like Morgan, Griffey, Foster, Pete Rose, etc. McCarver counseled me about the difference in left-handed batters in the National League compared to the American League. AL lefties tended to "bail and wail" or step toward first base and try to pull the ball because there weren't many Astroturf ballfields in the American League. So you pitched them away—not in. National League batters were the opposite. Because of the artificial turf and the speed they possessed, they could go the other way with pitches away from them. So McCarver said we have to pitch inside and jam them. It worked like a charm. My control was sharp. I navigated through six innings without giving up a run. I secured my spot in the rotation. But I was very ineffective that year. I started 27 games, but I won just six.

We were in Los Angeles in late July to play the Dodgers. Frank Jobe was the Dodgers' orthopedic surgeon and the inventor of the famous "Tommy John surgery." He was the pioneer. I asked our trainer Don Seger if he could arrange for me to see Dr. Jobe. Over the years I got to know Dr. Jobe quite well as the Dodgers trained in Vero Beach and I was living in Stuart, Florida. I'd go up and visit occasionally. Back in 1976 I walked over to the Dodgers' training room and met Dr. Jobe. I told him I didn't have any pain in my shoulder but that I had no life in my arm anymore. He put me through a few tests of resistance and rotations of my left arm. He asked me how many innings I had pitched. I did some rough math mentally and said about 4,000. He said I had some atrophy in my infraspinatus muscle. In layman's terms I had a loss of muscle strength in one of the four rotator cuff muscles located in the back of the armpit. What could I do to strengthen it? Weights were not used much in baseball at the time, but we had added a Nautilus machine, which was a circuit training device that used plates weighing from five pounds and up. Dr. Jobe suggested that I begin some internal and external rotations on the Nautilus machine using the five-pound weights.

Midway through the 1976 season, I began to do some exercises in the afternoon with Philadelphia Eagles Roman Gabriel, Bill Bergey, Herm Edwards, and others. I worked with their conditioning coach Gus Hoefling. I enjoyed it, and it was helpful. When Dick Vermeil took over the Eagles, he brought in his brother Al to be the conditioning coach, so Hoefling lost his job. Ruly Carpenter, the Phillies' owner at the time, was the best owner for a player of any team I played for in my entire career. Carpenter was in his late 30s, about my age. He played racquetball occasionally on the court at Veterans Stadium. I asked Carpenter to go through a set of Hoefling's exercises one day, and he agreed to hire him. Ruly's son, Bobby, became one of Hoefling's students and was the model in Hoefling's championship conditioning book. So with Hoefling's supervision, I began to do the exercises which Dr. Jobe had prescribed. Interestingly, on July 28 I pitched one of my best games of the year in that series, losing 2–1 to Tommy John of the Dodgers. That was my dead arm period before I began Dr. Jobe's exercise routine. I believe I am one of the first ballplayers to use a strength and conditioning coach.

I had a renewed hope in spring training of 1978 because of my offseason exercise program under Hoefling's supervision. Wade Wilson, son of my former teammate Ward Wilson, would come to our spring training complex and be my catcher for a few weeks prior to the official opening of spring training. After about 10 days of easy throwing, I began to ramp it up. He could already notice the life I had in my arm. The speed, movement, and spin were all a little better than in 1977.

I knew based on my performance the previous year that I was not going to be considered for a role as a starting pitcher. I'd maybe be a long relief man out of the bullpen who was used when the starter got knocked out early and the team was well behind. It was frustrating but understandable. I continued my program of throwing to a catcher off the bullpen mound every day to try to stay sharp just in case I was needed or if Ozark was desperate and had nobody else to use. Well, finally on April 25, the 13th game of the season, I got the call to start at home against the Chicago Cubs. I was as ready as one could be, having not started since late the previous season. My main concern was always control. But contrary to today's training methods, the everyday throwing I did helped me to have decent control. In a shocking result to most, I threw a nine-inning shutout, allowing just three hits with one walk.

I even knocked in a run. It was a step in the right direction for me.

I started again a few weeks later, but I didn't pitch well. I lost to the Reds but then began to get starts on a regular basis. Although I had pitched well, I seemed to come away with no decisions. I got my second decision of the season on June 4 for my second win. The complete-game effort came against the Dodgers and my good friend Tommy John. I got my record to 5–1 and ended the season at 8–5 with an ERA just north of 4.00. The year had an interesting finish. The Phillies had won 100 or more games in 1976 and 1977, but that year's team was not quite as strong. We had a comfortable lead over the Pirates after splitting a pair with them on September 11 and 12.

Tanner, who had been my manager a few years before in Chicago, was now the Pirates' skipper. He was the most positive-thinking manager on the planet. He was quoted as saying, "We are right where we want to be. I feel good about our team." Some of my Phillies teammates were mocking Tanner and asking me, "What has he been smoking?" But the Pirates won 13 of their next 16 games, and when we arrived at Three Rivers Stadium on September 29, our lead was down to three-and-a-half games before the start of a four-game series with the Pirates to finish the season. We played a doubleheader on Friday night and lost two one-run games. The Pirates scored the winning runs in the bottom of the ninth in both games, beating our ace Carlton 2–1. Our clubhouse went from loud to funereal. Tanner's prediction was getting close to reality. We still needed one more win to lock up the National League East.

Lerch, our promising young lefty, started for us. After one inning the Pirates led 4–1. It was quiet in our dugout. A loss would mean we would need to win, or Pittsburgh would have a tie-breaking game to play on Monday against us. And if the Pirates won that game, they would have overtaken us after being well behind all season. Well, Lerch, who was a good-hitting pitcher, homered in the second and the fourth off Don Robinson to make it 4–3. The Bull hit a three-run shot in the sixth to put us on top 6–5. We added four in the eighth and seemed pretty sure we would win the thing. But the Pirates kept clawing away and scored four in the bottom of the ninth before Reed struck out Willie Stargell and got Phil Garner to ground out with the tying runs on base. It was more relief than celebration in our clubhouse, but nevertheless we had won our third straight National League Eastern division title.

We lost the National League Championship Series to the Dodgers again and never got to the World Series with some of the best teams I was ever a part of in my 25 seasons, particularly the 1977 team. I regained a little credibility as a major league pitcher and enjoyed another offseason working out with Hoefling.

I knew that I wasn't in Ozark's plans in 1979, but I was on the staff and I kept to my throwing program. I asked bullpen coach Bob Tiefenauer if I could pitch some imaginary innings while we were batting to try to keep some rhythm and feel for the ball. I wanted to work on my spin, movement, touch, and feel. Ozark reluctantly agreed. I knew that my desire to stay sharp despite my not being used much was annoying him. He started me on April 24, and I was terrible. I only lasted two-plus innings against the Dodgers, issued five walks, and allowed three runs. It wasn't the runs which puzzled me. It was the walks. My days with the Phillies were coming to an end—and maybe my career, too.

But then I experienced some magic on May 8. We were getting thumped by Randy Jones and the Padres. Nothing new there. Jones always threw well against us. Their manager, Roger Craig, brought in their closer, future Hall of Famer Rollie Fingers, to start the seventh inning. I thought it was highly unusual for a closer to come in that early. The Padres led 7–3 going into the eighth inning. We made some noise in the eighth, scored two, and it was 7–5. We added another two in the ninth to tie the game. By this time, the only people left in our bullpen were Tiefenauer and me. Dave Rader, our third catcher, had gone in to pinch hit in the seventh. I had been throwing my dummy innings early in the game. And then as I saw that we were going to tie the game, I said to Tief, "I better get ready." But there was no call to the bullpen to say I was pitching. Although there was never a call to the bullpen or a signal from Ozark for me to come in, I was the only pitcher left. I just ran out to the bullpen mound and started throwing my warm-up pitches. I pitched three scoreless innings, and we scored two runs in the 13th. I gave up one in the bottom half, but we won 9–8, and I had a win in my last game as a Phillie. Ozark's words to me after the game were certainly an indication that he no longer wanted me around. "It's a good thing that you pitched well after all that throwing in the bullpen," he said.

I told him, "If I *hadn't* done all that throwing in the bullpen, I probably wouldn't have pitched as well!"

Three days later, I got a call from Owens. The Yankees had purchased my contract. Wow, the Bronx Bombers! Goose Gossage had just injured his finger in a clubhouse tussle with Cliff Johnson, who was always trying to pick a fight with someone. Sparky Lyle had been traded. They needed a lefty in the bullpen. Birdie Tebbetts had been a catcher for the Tigers and played for Detroit the day I saw my first big league games in 1946. By this time he was scouting for the Yankees and watched the game in San

Diego on May 8. He sent in a report that he thought I could help the Yankees.

We had a day game in San Francisco on May 11 and had scheduled our bridge dinner that night. We had eight people on the Phillies who were bridge players. We played for menial stakes but kept track of who owed the pot. Every six weeks or so, we'd go out for dinner, and the guys who owed the pot would buy. McCarver was our best player by far. Schmidt was the novice and least experienced and often sponsored the dinner. I had Eddie Ferenz, our traveling secretary, get me on a red-eye flight to New York. The Yankees were at home playing the Angels. I packed my suitcase and went to dinner with my bridge buddies: McCarver, Lonnie, Schmidtee, Maddux, and a few others. They toasted me and wished me well. We had been a close bunch of guys, veterans who stuck together. I arrived at LaGuardia Airport early on the 12th and thought I might as well go right to Yankee Stadium. I had no idea where to stay. I wound up staying at a Sheraton hotel in Hasbrouck Heights, New Jersey, where a lot of Yankees stayed before finding regular housing. The clubhouse was open, and I visited with "Big" Pete Sheehy, who was the clubhouse attendant since Babe Ruth's days with the team. His clubhouse rules: "What you see here, what you hear here, what you say here, let it stay here." Great advice!

Yankees manager Bob Lemon, a Hall of Fame pitcher, was in his office. I went in to introduce myself. "Welcome to the Zoo," were his first words. "Can you pitch today?" were his second.

"That's why I'm here," I said.

After my red-eye flight from the West Coast, I greeted my new teammates. I knew many of them already. For example, Graig Nettles and his wife, Ginger, had lived with us in September of 1967 when Nettles was called up and joined the Twins. Sheehy outfitted me with a uniform, and out to the bullpen I went.

In the top of the seventh inning, the Angels had runners on first and third with one out when Lem summoned me to come in and face my former teammate Carew. What a debut for the Yankees! I got him to ground into an inning-ending double play. We won the game 6–5. The rest of the season was the first time in my career that I was a full-time reliever. I appeared in 40 games and only pitched 58 innings. It was an inning here, there, and occasionally a little more.

A lot happened between mid-May and the end of the season. Yankees' owner George Steinbrenner replaced Lemon as manager with Martin. Nothing new there: Martin had managed the Yankees in all or parts of the previous four seasons.

Then, on August 2, tragedy struck. Thurman Munson was killed doing practice takeoffs and landings in Canton, Ohio. Munson had started flying in for games the past few years. With a lot of off days on Mondays and Thursdays, he could fly home after a game, spend a day and a half at home with his family, and then fly back for our next game. Munson's nickname was "Tugboat." It was probably given to him by Nettles, who had a quick wit and a sharp needle, because Munson was not known for his speed. He had flown home to Canton for the off day Thursday, August 2. After our game on July 31, I arranged an Italian dinner at Traverso's in Tinley Park, a suburb of Chicago, for several of the guys. Bucky Dent, Gossage, and I had become friends with the Traverso brothers a few years earlier when we played for the White Sox. The brothers were all fans of Munson's, and that's why I arranged the dinner. Munson was gracious enough to come along. A great time was had by all. Munson played first base the next night, and while we went to New York on the Yankees' charter, he flew home to Canton to practice takeoffs and landings with his new private jet.

I was subletting an apartment on 58th Street near 6th Avenue in Manhattan. After lunch I turned on the TV. I saw the shocking news that he had died in a plane crash. Along with everyone else, I was numb. Disbelief. *What do I do now?* The Yankees didn't have a phone number to reach me, and

I didn't have phone numbers for anyone on the team. I had friends from Florida who had just arrived in town. It was a sad and surreal couple of days. I reported to Yankee Stadium on Friday afternoon to find the distraught faces of Munson's teammates. He was my teammate now, too. I had pitched to him a few times during that season. He loved to say, "Kitty, we're going to pitch backward: slow stuff when you're behind in the count, fastballs when you're ahead."

I said, "Thurm, that's not backward; that's right thinking!"

At 40 I was certainly not a power pitcher, and hitters usually look for a fastball when the pitcher is behind in the count. When the pitcher is ahead in the count, batters expect you to try to get them out by getting them to chase your breaking stuff. So what Munson called "backward" was the right way to combat most hitters' thinking. He was a joy to pitch to as he loved to grin at me when we had fooled a good fastball hitter by sneaking a heater past him.

Steinbrenner addressed the team briefly until he was too overcome by emotion to finish. In 1976 Steinbrenner had named Munson as the Yankees' first captain since Lou Gehrig in 1939. The message was that after speaking to Diana, Thurman's wife, we were going to play that night. Big Pete had cleared out Munson's locker, and it was totally empty. No one would ever occupy it again. We played the next two nights in a daze while the national anthem was played with the catcher's spot left vacant in Munson's honor. It was decided that we would take a charter flight to Canton on Monday for Munson's memorial service and fly back to New York City after the service to play that night.

It was quite a day and quite a game. On our bus ride to the airport, people lined the streets with banners for Munson. It was the quietest bus ride I was ever on with a group of major league players. There was not the usual smack talk and revelry. In the game we trailed the Baltimore Orioles 4–0, going into the bottom of the seventh inning. Bobby Murcer, one of Munson's closest friends, hit a three-run home run to make it 4–3. Then, in the bottom of the ninth, Murcer did it again. With Dent on third and Willie Randolph on second, Murcer singled in the tying and the winning runs. We won 5–4, and Murcer had all five RBIs. What a fitting end to a very emotional game.

The rest of the season was a blur, and no one seemed to be in as competitive of a mood as when Tugboat was alive. Toward the end of the season, I asked Martin if he wanted me back next season. You never knew if Martin was shooting straight, but he said yes and told me to speak with Steinbrenner about next season's contract. My contract for 1979 was for $150,000. It was the contract I had signed with the Phillies. Cedric Tallis had the title of Yankees general manager, but Steinbrenner ran the show. I told Steinbrenner in his office that Martin wanted me back for 1980. He agreed. I didn't merit any raise because I didn't have much of a record with the Yankees but still had value as a lefty. A few years down the road, pitchers like me were called "LOOOGYs," short for Lefty Only One Out Guy. Steinbrenner agreed to a modest cost of living increase, which at 12 or 13 percent raised my deal to $169,000.

The offseason proved to be very interesting. Steinbrenner called me at my home in Glen Mills, Pennsylvania, in October and said as a paper transaction they wanted to remove me from the 40-man roster to protect one of their younger players from being claimed off the waiver list. He promised I would be back on the roster after the Winter Meetings and the waiver period had passed. I had never dealt with Steinbrenner before on a contract. He was relatively new to Major League Baseball. He had bought the Yankees in 1973. I knew he was eccentric and potentially volatile, but at that point, I had no reason to mistrust him. I didn't have or need an agent. I knew my real worth. If I wanted to continue to pitch in the majors I couldn't price myself out of the market.

CHAPTER 4

The 1980s

G ene Michael had been named the New York Yankees general manager. "Stick," as he was called because he was tall and thin, sent me a letter in early January that said that the Yankees were inviting me to spring training as a non-rostered player with an opportunity to make the team. I was puzzled. So I called Stick. We had played against each other a few times when I was with the Minnesota Twins, and he was a shortstop and second baseman with the Yankees. "What's going on, Stick?" I asked.

George Steinbrenner and I had agreed on a contract back in October, and he promised to put me on the 40-man roster. That was important because if the Yankees released me at some point, they'd still have to honor my contract for the full $169,000—chump change for the Yankees and about a fourth of today's minimum salary. Stick called Steinbrenner, who said he did not remember our conversation. Welcome to the Bronx Zoo and dealing with George Steinbrenner!

I called and asked to speak with Steinbrenner. His administrative assistant said that she'd put me on a call list, and he might call me back later in the day. I told her that I'd rather be put on hold. I was in no hurry. It wasn't too long before Steinbrenner picked up. I asked him about the deal we had made. He said he kept recordings of all his phone conversations and had no record of that one. I told him: "George, we met *in person*, and I remember distinctly what you promised."

He continued to deny it and he had me over a barrel. At the time the offseason free-agent draft allowed a player who filed for free agency to be drafted by up to 11 clubs. That ship had sailed for me. I believe that a club would have picked me up just on my reputation, and that my lefty-on-lefty role was a specialty more teams desired. An indication that I think Steinbrenner *knew* he was lying to me was the fact that he immediately said that he would give me an additional $5,000 for spring training expenses. They paid basic room and board for players and incidental money, but this was a nice bonus.

In the meantime, Billy Martin was fired because of a barroom scuffle with a marshmallow salesman. Dick Howser was the new manager—my fourth different manager in less than a year. I knew Howser. He was a classy guy. I met with him as soon as I got to Fort Lauderdale, Florida, where the Yankees trained. I told Howser that I was there because Martin said he thought I'd be helpful as a lefty-on-lefty guy. If he had different ideas, I didn't want to waste his time or mine. I would make some calls and try to hook on with somebody. I felt very confident that I could still get big league hitters out. Howser said, "I will give you every chance I can to make the team."

The Yankees' team doctor was Dr. Dan Kanell. I was renting a condo Doc owned, and we became good friends. He was about my size, and many thought we resembled each other. So, one morning, Doc knocked on my door of the condo. He said "Kitty, we had an organizational meeting last night, and the team decided to put Rudy May on the disabled list at the start of the season. They'll have to carry you for at least the first month."

May was a hard-throwing lefty and had a very good year for the Yankees in 1980 (15–5 with a league-leading ERA of 2.46). The next day, Stick approached me on the field and said "George gave me a contract for you to sign." We walked over to a bench on the side of the field, and I read the contract.

I said, "This is for $150,000. George had agreed to $169,000." Stick went back to Steinbrenner with my request, and Steinbrenner was not happy.

"He either signs that, or the deal is off," he said. "I'll find somebody else."

I signed for $150,000, appeared in four games, pitched five innings, and absorbed one loss. I did not pitch effectively at all. My last appearance for the Yankees was against the Chicago White Sox on April 17. I gave up three runs in one inning. The ax fell shortly after that outing. May was ready to pitch, and Stick informed me that I was being designated for assignment. That meant that any team had 10 days to assume my contract and acquire me, or I was a free agent. I said good-bye to my teammates and headed to my farm in Glen Mills, Pennsylvania. I just walked around talking to my horses, Standardbred trotters, and pondered my next move. On the eighth day of my DFA period, John Claiborne, the general manager of the St. Louis Cardinals, called me to ask whether I could be in St. Louis by noon the following day, as the Cardinals had a day game, and they had just assumed my contract. I said, "John, in two days I'll be a free agent. The Yankees would have to pay me for the year, and any team could sign me for the minimum salary," which at the time was just $30,000. The average salary that year was a little more than $143,000.

John said, "We need help in the bullpen *right now!*"

I said, "John, you know you're not talking to Goose Gossage, don't you?" He laughed.

Here is a bigger laugh. I caught an early morning flight from Philadelphia to St. Louis and arrived at Busch Stadium a little after noon. The game had already started. It was a 12:00 "businessman's special" time for first pitch. As I walked into the clubhouse, Darold Knowles, a veteran lefty, was walking out. The Cardinals had just DFA-ed him. He said, *"You're the* kid that's taking my place?" We both laughed. I was two years older than Knowles.

The Cardinals had a comfortable 8–0 lead over the Chicago Cubs after seven innings, and I asked bullpen coach Dave Ricketts if I could throw a little. I hadn't held a baseball in my hand for almost two weeks. He got the okay from Cardinals manager Ken Boyer, so I started warming up. The Cubs put a couple men on in the eighth, scored a run, and were threatening to score more when the bullpen phone rang. Boyer asked if I could pitch in the game. *Really? Sure, I'm ready!*

When I went to the mound, Pete Vukovich looked at me and said, "When did you get here?"

I said, "About noon today. I'm your new teammate!" He didn't even know I was on the team. He chuckled and walked to the dugout.

I asked Terry Kennedy, our catcher, what sign we were using. I don't remember, but it usually was one for a fastball, two for a curve, three for a slider, and a wiggle of the fingers for a change-up. We kept things pretty simple in those days. My approach was always down and away with a fastball, occasionally one up and in, and get breaking pitches over when you're behind in the count. I don't recall the exact sequence I used, but four of the five hitters I faced grounded out, and one struck out. The next day I faced seven men. I retired five on ground-outs and two on strikeouts for a save. Most of my pitches were down and away. I was now a member of my third different team in less than a year. I saved the next game, and suddenly the Cardinals thought, *maybe he* is *Goose Gossage!*

I saved Vuck's next start and added a couple more by the end of the season. My season highlight came on June 8. Gussie Busch fired the popular Boyer. Whitey Herzog was now our manager. The Cardinals found out I was not Gossage as I lost three games in relief, but John Fulgham had injured his shoulder, and Herzog asked me if I'd like to start. *Of course I would.* So after not having pitched more than four innings in a game in more than a year, I started against the New York Mets at Shea Stadium on June 4. After a few innings, Claude Osteen, our pitching coach, started asking me after every inning how I felt. I kept saying fine. By the way, Osteen had been my teammate and golf buddy five years earlier when we were both with the White Sox. The result was a 1–0 win as Kenny Reitz hit a home run off Neil Allen in the top of the 10th inning. Wow, I was a starter again!

I started 14 games in 1980, completed six, and was 8–4 in my starts. At my age—41 at the time—and with my relationship with Herzog, I just made an appointment to go in and talk to him about 1981. It was a simple negotiation. I just asked him if he thought I could still pitch and help the team. He said yes and added that he wanted me to be his lefty-on-lefty guy, as Steve Mingori was with the Kansas City Royals. The Royals had been very successful when Herzog was their manager, and he was the best I'd seen operating a bullpen. Herzog always had a knack of getting relievers in against hitters they had a good chance of getting out.

Selfishly, I still wanted to be a starter and I knew I could do well as a starter, but I felt obligated to take on the role Herzog suggested. Wise choice. At the time, Herzog was in the unique position of being both the field manager *and* the general manager of the Cardinals. He signed me to a nice contract with a base of $160,000 with bonuses for appearing in a certain amount of games. I never reached the bonus numbers because of the 50-day strike (June 12–August 9) in 1981, but Herzog gave me the $35,000 anyway.

The 1981 season was marred by that strike. The owners were trying to get the players to give up free agency, but that wasn't going to happen. I pleaded with then-commissioner Bowie Kuhn to use his "best interest of baseball" authority to get the issue resolved. I said that if anyone would vote against striking, it would be me. At age 42 I was never going to play long enough to make up for the money I lost because of the strike. I told him, "The players will not bend, and you know that."

Kuhn and I got along well as we met during the early negotiations between the players and owners when he was the

National League attorney, and Bob Allison and I were player representatives for the Twins. It was a futile action by the owners, but they had strike insurance for 50 days. We settled on the 51st day and were back to the status quo. Because of the strike we played a split season. The Cardinals had the overall best winning percentage in the National League East but finished second in both halves. The Philadelphia Phillies and Montreal Expos were the division winners.

Meanwhile, my career as a broadcaster started to gain some momentum. During the strike of 1981, I broadcast some Triple A games with Hall of Famer Ralph Kiner and Warner Fusselle. Jodi Shapiro was the executive producer of HTS (Home Team Sports) out of Washington, D.C. At the time there was no major league team in Washington. The station had been broadcasting the Baltimore Orioles games, but with the major league players on strike, they decided to do some games of their Triple A team, the Rochester Red Wings. The shortstop was Cal Ripken Jr., and their star pitcher was Mike Boddicker. I did about 10 games during the strike and then went back to playing when the strike ended. Shapiro had shown interest in me as a baseball analyst when I was with the Phillies and heard me do interviews during rain delays with Richie Ashburn and Harry Kalas.

The next season, 1982, was a magical year and also my last full season as a major league pitcher. I pitched well enough in

1981 that Herzog wanted me back again and said he would build his 1982 staff from the ninth inning back. We obtained Bruce Sutter, a future Hall of Fame closer. We had acquired what modern-day baseball people call "pieces." I dislike that term. I know that nobody means anything impersonal when they say it, but players are *not* pieces. They're *people*.

Late in 1981 we got Doug Bair, and at the start of 1987, we got Jeff Lahti. They were a pair of right-handed pitchers from the Cincinnati Reds and a big part of our bullpen in 1982. Lahti had a sharp slider and had a knack for getting the first batter out when he came in with runners on base. He did that 36 out of 37 times. Bair was an over-the-top pitcher who relied on his fastball. I was the LOOOGY (Lefty for One Out Only Guy). And Sutter was the closer with his effective revolutionary split-finger fastball that dipped out of the zone and was close to unhittable in many games.

It was such a fun team to be a part of. We hit 67 home runs as a team and stole 200 bases. Herzog's battle cry every game was "Get me 10 singles!" Lonnie Smith, Willie McGee, Ozzie Smith, or Tommy Herr would turn a single into a double or a triple. We also had terrific defense. One thing that doesn't show up in a box score or stat sheet is when a left fielder like Lonnie Smith chases down a hit near the left-field foul line and gets it to the second baseman quickly enough to hold the batter to a single. A play like that keeps the double play in play, and we turned many of those. That changes the entire game in our favor.

When we played the Phillies, I stayed at my farmhouse in Glen Mills and rode to the game with my friend and former teammate Mike Schmidt. He told me how dangerous the Expos were because of their power, speed, and good pitching. I told him, "You better worry about us. We have speed, defense, and Bruce Sutter!"

We had a key three-game series against the Phillies in mid-September and beat them two out of three. Two weeks later, we clinched the National League East division with a win at Montreal. Pitching, defense, and speed were a great combination. During the regular season, the Atlanta Braves had beaten us in seven out of 12 games. But we thought that the Braves got a lot of good breaks when they played us. We swept them in the National League Championship Series (a best-of-five affair at the time) and were on our way to the World Series to face the Milwaukee Brewers. I learned from my first World Series in 1965 about how to deal with the excitement. You have to make sure not to get distracted by the ticket requests, family, and other logistics. I got a room in a grade B motel not far from Busch Stadium in St. Louis and kept to myself. If I had done that in 1965, I might have performed better in Game Five.

We got blitzed by Mike Caldwell, Paul Molitor, and the Brewers 9–0 in Game One. Then we won Games Two and Three. I made cameo appearances in the first four games, and I had three good performances and one bad. The Brewers came back in Games Four and Five to take a 3–2 lead in the World Series. On the way back to St. Louis after Game Five, I spent a little time speaking with John Stuper, our starter for Game Six. I told Stuper a couple of things. First, no one expects you to outpitch Don Sutton, who is a future Hall of Famer. Second, we have won two straight a lot more times than we have lost three straight. I told him to try to treat Game Six like a 10:00 AM spring practice game. That's easy to say, tougher to do.

Stuper pitched a complete game, one of the great Game Six performances in World Series history. We won 13–1 before nearly 54,000 fans and knocked Sutton out in the fifth inning. Catcher Darrell Porter, the World Series MVP (from Sugar Creek, Missouri, just 230 miles from St. Louis), and first baseman Keith Hernandez each hit two-run homers and built a comfortable lead for Stuper. But the impressive part was that Stuper pitched through a few rain delays and kept going out to the mound after the delays. The game was clocked at two hours and 21 minutes, but it actually took more than five hours to complete.

That meant it was on to Game 7. We came back with some late-game magic and won 6–3. The highlight was my teammate and now longtime-friend Hernandez getting the game-tying hit off Brewers lefty Bob McClure. He and Hernandez had been teammates in sandlot ball, high school ball, and American Legion baseball in the Bay Area. What a moment for these two friends! McClure now lives five minutes from me in Stuart, Florida.

My all-time top moment in baseball happened when Sutter struck out "Stormin'" Gorman Thomas to end the game and make the Cardinals world champions. In my 25th year in the majors, I was going to earn my first World Series ring.

With two outs in the ninth inning, St. Louis police came over to our bullpen down the right-field line and asked if we would like to go sit in the dugout because they anticipated bedlam after the final out. Dave Ricketts, our bullpen coach, and I stayed. I said I'd been waiting too long for this moment. I'm staying right here to soak it up. It was bedlam, and on my way in to join the celebration, I was bumped, jostled, and stepped on, but it was worth every bit of it.

Our bullpen didn't have the highest percentage of holding leads when leading after six innings, but we held the lead after seven innings more than any team in the National League. We held the lead after six innings in 80 games, and our record was 69–11. We held the lead after seven innings in 83 games, and our record was 74–9. That points out how important it is to score early and have the lead late.

It wasn't a raucous parade through the Canyon of Heroes such as the New York teams experience, but it was a parade through St. Louis, the best baseball town in America. St. Louis doesn't have the feel of a major city like the bigger East Coast cities, but it is a great baseball town. The Cardinals baseball team is the favorite professional sports team of the St. Louis fans. Yes, the city loves the Blues and did love the football Cardinals and Rams and the NBA's Hawks (long ago), but they have always been fanatical about their baseball team.

The city was a sea of red for the parade. Everyone was bundled up as if it were winter. October 27 in St. Louis can be chilly. Red is usually the dominant color of apparel when the Cardinals have a home game. We rode in the back of red trucks and slapped hands and waved to everyone along the streets. I had imagined for many years how that might feel, and it was exhilarating to be part of a group that accomplished everything it set out to do back in February.

And then it was over. There was a team gathering later that day, and then it was off to our winter homes until next February.

It was a disappointing offseason as things ended unceremoniously. My 1982 salary was $200,000. The minimum at the time was $33,000 and change. The average salary was $241,000. So after contributing in a small but important role to the success we had, I thought I deserved more than the average big league salary. It was my 25th season in the majors, making me the longest-tenured player in history. That's heady stuff. My friend and former, teammate Tommy John, eventually passed me by a year, and then Hall of Famer Nolan Ryan passed him by a year.

Holds were not an official statistic at the time. In my opinion, they still shouldn't be. It's a bogus stat. You can give up runs and still get credited with a hold. My job was to get a lefty hitter out late in the game and keep the lead. I did that a high percentage of the time. My teammates knew that. I don't need a phony stat to validate it.

With Herzog dishing off the general manager's job to Joe McDonald, a friend and colleague from Herzog's Mets days, negotiations would prove to be very different and very acrimonious. After the parade and celebration, I had asked Herzog whether he wanted me back in 1983. He said, "Absolutely. Go work out a contract with Joe." I didn't hear from McDonald, and it was now mid-January, so I called him. I was shocked by his reply.

"We haven't decided what we'll do this season yet," he said. "We're thinking about Andy Hassler, a veteran lefty." And he mentioned a few other names.

I said in a somewhat loud voice, "Are you serious? Have you discussed this with Whitey? He told me last fall that he wanted me back this season."

After a few back-and-forth, contentious phone calls, he agreed to send me a contract. At first, he was going to invite me to spring training as a non-rostered player. So my case to McDonald was that the average for a veteran reliever in the major leagues was over $500,000. I certainly didn't expect a raise of that magnitude, but I thought a contract of $300,000 was reasonable as we had just won the World Series and drawn over two million fans. So McDonald went to Herzog and told him that I was asking for $500,000, which was a straight-up lie. And then Herzog sent me a letter questioning my motive. He said that he wanted me back but that I couldn't be asking for that kind of money. I wrote back to Herzog (in the days before text and email) and told him that McDonald was lying. I don't think Herzog wanted to hear that.

Meanwhile, my dad was on his deathbed in Zeeland, Michigan. He had suffered a stroke 15 years before, and his life was about to end. So I drove to Michigan to see him and spend as much time with him as I could. That was during a period of time when winter baseball banquets were held. As a member of our 1982 championship team, I was invited to attend. I wrote to Marty Henden, our public relations person extraordinaire, and told him I would be unable to go because of my dad's deteriorating health. I received another letter from Herzog saying that he was disappointed that I skipped the baseball writers' dinner because of my contract dispute, a misunderstanding that was another lie from McDonald.

When all was said and done, I signed a contract for $285,000 with a clause adding $15,000 if the Cards drew 2.3 million or more fans in 1983. We could have gotten this done so much more civilly and less acrimoniously, but a lot of general managers liked to beat the players in negotiations. McDonald was one of those, I guess. He was without a doubt the most dishonest, unethical baseball executive I had ever dealt with my 25 major league seasons. If McDonald and I met on the street today, we would greet each other and be pleasant to each other. As with a lot of the old-school general managers, it wasn't personal. It was the way they treated players before free agency, which is why we fought hard to get free agency and why players will continue to fight hard to keep it.

I could already tell in spring training that things were a bit frosty between Herzog and me. When I stepped on to the field on Opening Day, April 5, 1983, I became the last major leaguer who had played in the 1950s. By the end of my career on July 1 of that year, I was also the last active original Washington Senators player. The '83 season began, and when the bullpen phone rang, I expected the call to be for me. But it was for Dave Von Ohlen, "The Baron." I liked him a lot. We would spend time together after spring workouts having a bite to eat and a cold beer. A lefty whom the Cardinals acquired from the Mets, he was a good guy, and I felt no animosity toward him. But I began to see what was happening. I was being phased out.

We had a few injuries to our pitching staff and we were headed west to play the San Francisco Giants and the San Diego Padres, who both had several left-handed batters, which gave me hope. So I returned to my farm in Glen Mills and relaxed during the All-Star break. I was sitting out by the pool when my daughter called to say, "There's a man named Joe McDonald on the phone."

McDonald said very succinctly and in a business-like way, "We just acquired Dave Rucker from Detroit and we are releasing you." I was stunned for a moment, trying to think of something to say. What followed seemed like several minutes of silence, but it was probably just a few seconds.

I finally said, "Well, Joe, I don't think this conversation will get any more pleasant. So I'll just say good-bye and go back to St. Louis to gather my belongings."

Back at the pool, I stared into space for a while. And it hit me: I had played Major League Baseball longer than any other pitcher. Commissioner Kuhn had given me a plaque attesting to that. I had been playing baseball in the summer my entire adult life—professionally for 27 seasons. I was now 44 years old, and with that two-minute phone call, my career as a player was over.

I soon got over the sentimentality of it. It was time to get up and get going. Off to St. Louis I went. The team had left for San Diego to start the second half, so no one was around the clubhouse. I gathered up my baseball gear, went to the apartment I was renting, got my personal belongings, and headed back to Philadelphia. I did make a few calls to see if anyone might be in the market for a 44-year-old lefty to get an out or two late in the game. That would be hard for them to accept. I wasn't Sandy Koufax. I was a normal lefty whom they could easily replace with a younger arm. Mike Krukow, a friend who was then pitching for the Giants, had manager Tom Haller call me to see if I wanted to finish the season with them. Kruk thought I could be a good influence for their younger pitchers. I thought long and hard about that, but I didn't want to be jumping from club to club just to hang on. I asked Haller if he could promise to take me to spring training in 1984 at age 45. He couldn't do that, which I understood.

I went to visit the Cardinals when they came to Philadelphia to play the Phillies in August. I learned a good lesson that I have since passed on to many players. I could sense that I was no longer part of the team when I saw guys hustling to get on the field, caught up in their pregame routines. Not that they were unpleasant or unfriendly, but they had a job to do. Herzog passed me and said, "Oh, I'm sorry I didn't get a chance to call you. I was really busy with the All-Star Game activities." Because the Cardinals were the defending National League champs, Herzog was the manager of the National League team.

As time went on, I thought that was as classless a move as I had ever seen by such a respected organization. But I remembered what I had told my friend and former teammate Harmon Killebrew years ago. After one of my many contract battles with Twins owner Calvin Griffith, Killer said to me: "Jim, if you don't give Calvin such a battle with your contract every year, he'll take care of you after your playing career is over."

My answer, which he later told me was correct, was: "Harm, when you stop hitting the ball over the wall, they won't know how to spell your name." Killebrew, who was one of the most popular and revered athletes in Minnesota history, was released by the Twins in January of 1975. Griffith offered Killebrew the job of Triple A hitting coach for an annual salary of $7,500. Instead, Killebrew opted to sign with the Royals for the 1975 season and finished his career there. The Royals released him after that season. I told him at an event later: "So the Cardinals built a statue of Stan Musial, and the Twins offered you the Triple A hitting coach job."

The lesson is: you leave on your own terms or you are at the mercy of your employer's terms. Fortunately for Killebrew and other Twins greats, the current ownership has erected statues to honor Rod Carew, Kent Hrbek, Tony Oliva, Kirby Puckett, and Killebrew.

I knew I would get some calls from the media regarding the apparent end of my career. I disciplined myself to take the high road. I constantly said I felt fortunate to have been able to play in the major leagues for as long as I did. I considered it a great 25-year vacation. Not many get to dream about being a big leaguer as a young boy and then do it until age 44. I honestly felt that way but still thought it was totally unlike a class organization such as the Cardinals to handle the end of my career the way they did. That would never happen today. Some players play fewer than 10 years, and teams hold a press conference to announce their retirement.

So I began to pursue some broadcasting opportunities. I went to the Winter Meetings in Nashville after the 1983 season. Wally Phillips, a legendary radio icon on WGN in Chicago, was a big fan of mine and he reached out and asked if I'd like to do some reports for him from there. I also did some for a Philadelphia station. While I was there, I ran in to Chuck Tanner and Pete Peterson. Tanner was then managing the Pittsburgh Pirates, and Peterson was their general manager. They both said, "You look like you can still pitch." I answered that I knew I could still pitch, but it's not easy to convince a team to take on a 45 year old ahead of their young talent.

Tanner suggested that I come to spring training in Bradenton, Florida, with the Pirates next spring. "Pete will draw up a contract contingent on you making the team," he said. "We'll get you as many appearances as we can and get you some exposure to other teams." That sounded good to me. I had no other plans.

I had a good time in Bradenton. Willie Stargell was still there. A thin, young player with a big smile named Bobby Bonilla was there. Dave Parker had been traded so they assigned me No. 39, which had been Parker's number. The Pirates had an abundance of left-handed relievers: Rod Scurry, Dave Tomlinson, and Chris Green. I knew there was not much chance of hooking on with the Pirates, but Tanner did pitch me against the Boston Red Sox a few times. I did well. I got Jim Rice and Dewey Evans out.

On March 25 clubs had to make a decision about non-roster players: sign them or allow them freedom to sign elsewhere. So Tanner suggested that I call Lou Gorman, the general manager of the Red Sox. They needed a lefty reliever. Boston had acquired John Henry Johnson, a young lefty who had a live arm but seemed to be injured a lot.

Gorman was cordial, and I made my case. He asked, "How old are you now?"

I said, "45, Lou. But I can assure you that if I'm on the disabled list, you don't have to pay me. Sign me to a contract for the minimum, and I can help you."

Gorman opted to keep Johnson, who *did* get injured. He appeared in only 30 games, and the Red Sox released him after the season. At age 31 his career was over. Gorman and I laughed about it later. I kidded him about missing out on a durable 45 year old in exchange for a fragile young pitcher. Gorman's standard line after a conversation was usually, "Let's have lunch."

In 1984 I called Ellen Beckwith of ESPN to see if she might need me on the college games they carried. I broadcast a few of them in the first part of 1984 and I worked the College World Series (Arizona State vs. Oklahoma State) in Omaha. That's where I learned a lot about the mechanics of putting baseball games on TV from Fred Gaudelli, who is now the producer of NBC's *Sunday Night Football*. He's a rock star in the industry. He had me sit in the TV truck and watch what went on in there during a game. It was maddening. Baseball moves slowly, but in the production truck, things happen at warp speed. That was valuable time for me. I thanked Gaudelli many times for what he taught me.

In August I was on my way to Saratoga Springs, New York, to watch the Travers Stakes horse race with a trainer named "Lofty" Bruce when I heard on the radio that Pete Rose had been named to manage the Cincinnati Reds. I said to Lofty, "I'm going to get a call tomorrow. Pete is going to ask me to be his pitching coach." I told him how a few years ago he sent the Phillies batting practice pitcher over to tell me that if he ever got a managing job, he wanted me to be his pitching coach. I was flattered. Lofty said that Rose had probably made that promise to a lot of guys. "No," I said, "He'll call me." And he did.

Rose left a message at my home in Glen Mills. I rented a car and headed home. I called him and told him I had some unique ideas on coaching pitchers—different from the norm. They were things Johnny Sain had taught me. "Kitty," Rose said, "I know hitting, not pitching. You're free to do anything you wish with the pitchers."

The position sounded like it would be a lot of fun. And it was. I joined the Reds on August 24 in Pittsburgh. Jeff Russell, a promising young right-hander, shut out the Pirates 2–0 on three hits. The next day was my first pregame pitchers' meeting. I told them it would probably be the shortest meeting of this kind that they had ever had. It wasn't complicated. I used to call them "scare the pitchers" meetings. When they were finished, pitchers were afraid to throw the ball over the plate for fear that a batter could hit every pitch they threw. I quickly articulated my philosophy: "Pitch hitters high and tight or low and away. Get your secondary pitches over when you're behind in the count. The most important pitch is strike one. The second most important is strike two. We shade pull hitters a step to pull; everyone else is straight away. Abner Doubleday put the players there for a good reason. Go get 'em." That was it. The pitchers loved that approach.

The Reds finished in fifth place that season—22 games behind the Padres. Part of my duties was to go to Tampa and work with young pitchers in the Instructional League, an offseason league used for developmental purposes. It was designed to provide the young prospects more exposure and experience in hopes of speeding up their climb to the majors. I told the young pitchers how much my own time in the Instructional League had helped me. Harry Dorish, a former major league pitcher, was the Reds' minor league pitching coach. I'm sure that I had Dorish's trading card when I was a boy. He told me how much I was going to like a young pitcher named Tom Browning, a lefty who worked quickly, threw strikes, and had no fear. Brownie and I hit it off immediately. Browning was a dream for a pitching coach and a team. I was in Korea covering Olympic baseball for NBC with Jay Randolph when Browning pitched his perfect game for the Reds against the Los Angeles Dodgers on September 16, 1988.

Browning went 20–9, and the Reds improved to 89–72 in 1985. The last time a rookie pitcher won 20 games was when Bob Grim won 20 for the Yankees in 1954. We finished second to the Dodgers in 1985, and improved pitching was a big part of that. I liked a four-man rotation of three days' rest between starts. It kept you sharp and kept your arm rested just the right amount between starts: 72 hours. It's been proven that 72 hours is enough time for muscles to recover from maximum use from pitching. Thus three days between starts is ideal to keep a starting pitcher sharp and strong. John Franco and Ted Powers were our closers. Veteran Mario Soto and young pitchers like Ron Robinson and my former teammate, Stuper, contributed as well.

I really enjoyed coaching, but it was more involved and time-consuming than pitching—and for a paltry wage compared to playing. Bob Howsam, the Reds' veteran general manager, said, "We don't pay our coaches a big wage, but they get service time toward their pension."

I said, "Bob, a player needs only 10 years as a major leaguer to get their full pension. I have 25 years of service time as a player."

Howsam said, "Jim, I know you don't have any experience as a pitching coach, so this will be totally new to you."

I humbly replied with a bit of sarcasm, "Bob, I hope that my 25 years as a major league pitcher and learning ideas from a lot of coaches will help me do that job." The pitching coach's annual salary was $45,000. I said, "Bob, I'm taking this job for one reason: I'm honored and humbled that a person of Pete Rose's baseball knowledge and experience wants me to be his pitching coach."

It was a rewarding year and a half. The things I learned from Sain were very useful in coaching the Reds' pitchers. I would leave it to someone who spoke with my pitchers to judge whether I did a good job. My biggest devotee is Stuper. After his four years in the majors with the Cardinals and the Reds, he went on to coach at Yale for 25 years. He still uses some of the training methods I used coaching him with the Reds in 1985.

Near the end of 1985, my friend Tim McCarver asked me whether I had any interest in the broadcast business. His agent, Bob Rosen, indicated that he thought that I had a future as a broadcaster. He offered to represent me. After speaking with Rosen, McCarver, and my friend Jack McAleese, an attorney whom McCarver and I leaned on for advice, I decided to try broadcasting. I gave a nice year-end party for my pitchers (Soto, Jay Tibbs, Andy McGaffigan, Stuper, Robinson, Joe Price, Frank Pastore, Franco, Tom Hume, Carl Willis, Power, Bob Buchanan, Rob Murphy, and Mike Smith) at The Precinct, a popular restaurant/bar where a lot of the local sports crowd hung out in Cincinnati. I gave out funny little awards to each of them. The pitchers enjoyed it and so did I.

I was only leaving to go into the broadcasting business because at the time the owners and general managers acted like they were doing you a favor by giving you a coaching job. I had told Rose that if I could get a multi-year contract for some respectable money—like something in the six-figure range—I would love to keep coaching. But Marge Schott was the Reds' owner, so that was not happening. I would have a better chance of getting $100,000 per year to take care of her St. Bernard, Schottzie, than to coach her pitchers. She occasionally brought Schottzie on to the field. Tufts of Schottzie's hair would get all over us when we were near him.

So I found an apartment in New York City to sublease for the winter months' job hunting. Lo and behold, Joe DeAmbrosio, the Yankee public relations director, tracked me down and told me that Don Carney, the producer of Yankee broadcasts on WPIX-TV, was trying to reach me. Carney had heard me do several interviews and rain delay stints. Without even looking at a demo tape, Carney offered me a job on one condition: the station needed the approval of Yankees' owner George M. Steinbrenner. I said, "Good luck with that!"

But much to my surprise, Steinbrenner welcomed me to the team. My mentor, Bill White, warned me about what Steinbrenner required: he would send notes down to me during broadcasts—but never to Bill White or to Phil "Scooter" Rizzuto—to criticize the umpires or threaten to file a complaint with the commissioner. White told me, "Never compromise your credibility. Throw those notes in the trash basket. You are not a real Yankee. You'll probably be here only for a year, so do it right. If I weren't Black, he would have fired me years ago!"

I carried that motto of never compromising my credibility during my entire broadcasting career with me and still do. Rizzuto, a Brooklyn native who was inducted into the Baseball Hall of Fame in 1994, was the Yankees' shortstop from 1941 to 1942 and then 1946 to 1956. When Tony Kubek came along, Scooter went right from the diamond to the broadcast booth. White played mostly at first base for the San Francisco Giants, St. Louis Cardinals, and Philadelphia Phillies in 1956 and 1958–1969. Each brought a wealth of baseball experience to the broadcasts. White became a very close friend and a mentor as far as dealing with Yankee management.

I learned to do a little play-by-play with help from Rizzuto. We had a three-man rotation. On a very cold April night in Cleveland, Scooter and I were broadcasting the final three innings. White was free to go and get out of the cold. As I sat in the booth during a commercial break, Scooter, who addressed everyone by their last name, said, "Kaat, I need to go to the john." He wasn't back by the time the inning started, so I had no choice but to start in with whoever the Indians' batter was and away I went. Carney shouted through the talk-back channel, which didn't go over the air, "Where's Rizzuto?" I hit my talkback button and said, "He went to the john" and then quickly back to the game. Rizzuto never came back. He went to the warmth of the hotel room. I found out later that Scooter had a habit of doing that—leaving before the game was over.

Leavitt Pope, the president of WPIX, wanted to sign me to a multi-year deal, but Steinbrenner wouldn't approve it. He had fired Martin as manager and needed a spot for him, so he used that as an excuse not to re-sign me. The real reason was I was too honest and objective for him—not Yankees-biased enough. That actually was a blessing, which rewarded me years later. I think the reason I later was accepted by viewers in the New York market is because I was not a homer.

I was also blessed away from the field in 1986. I met MaryAnn Montanaro in Boca Raton, Florida, which was near the Yankees spring training headquarters in Fort Lauderdale. We spent the 1986 season together in New York, and it was apparent that we were in love and good for each other. We were married in 1988 and spent 22 wonderful years together until she passed away from bladder cancer in 2008.

In 1987 I had no full-time broadcasting job. I was asked to be the president of the fledgling Major League Baseball

Players Alumni Association. A group of former Washington Senators decided to start it. Jim Hannan, a Notre Dame grad and a bright guy, along with Fred Valentine, Chuck Hinton, and Frank Kreutzer, were all original members. There were a few others as well. They asked if I would devote some time to running the organization from their offices in Leesburg, Virginia. I agreed.

In the meantime spring training was going on, and my friend Sutter was with the Braves, who trained in West Palm Beach, Florida. Sutter invited me down to visit over a cold beer. As we were visiting, Sutter asked what I was going to do during the upcoming season. I told him about the alumni association gig. Glenn Diamond, the executive producer of Braves games on TBS, overheard me. He asked if I'd like to announce some games on the Braves Network. John Sterling was one of the Braves' announcers, but he also announced games for the Atlanta Hawks in the NBA. Since the Hawks made the playoffs, Sterling would probably miss close to 20 Braves games. *Voila!* I now had a part-time announcing gig to go along with my alumni gig.

Being president of the Major League Baseball Players Alumni Association was not a salaried position. They had enough funds to pay my expenses—rent and a little food money. The alumni had three employees or four counting a part-time secretary. I soon found out that all the money generated from charity golf events was going to pay the salaries of the full-time employees, and not much was going to charities. This rankled Joe Garagiola, who was involved with the Baseball Assistance Team (BAT), an organization formed by commissioner Peter Ueberroth. Its purpose was to help former players who had medical issues or who had fallen on hard times. BAT would help anyone who had a problem except a problem with illicit drugs.

Without airing all the back-and-forth discussions, I made a suggestion to the alumni board that they hire Dan Foster, one of the three full-time employees of the Major League Baseball Players Association, and let the others go. The main function of the alumni association at the time was to hold a few charity golf tournaments in several cities, and those would be hosted by a former big leaguer and supported mainly by Budweiser. In 1987 we had fewer than 100 members and were on the brink of becoming extinct. Today the alumni association has more than 6,000 members, and Foster has been the executive director for almost 30 years. They have raised millions for charity. I am proud to have been part of the resurrection, but most of the credit goes to Foster and the founders.

Anyhow, Diamond laid out a schedule for me, and I got to work with Skip Caray, Pete Van Wieren, and Ernie Johnson. All were good guys and very helpful in my learning the craft.

After I worked 20 games, Rex Lardner, the vice president of broadcasting for the network, wanted to sign me for a full-time position. Up until then, it was mostly a White man's arena. Lardner said that Ted Turner, who owned the Braves and TBS, had told him to seek out and hire a minority to join the announcing team. They hired Billy Sample, a friend and a good guy. I auditioned for the Cubs' vacancy and they hired Dave Nelson, also a friend and a good guy. But as was the case with a lot of my career, when one door closed behind me, another one opened.

In 1988 I was invited to join the Twins broadcast team. I announced Twins games for the next six years, and that was special to me because it was my original organization. The Twins were coming off a world championship season, and fan interest was high again in the Twin Cities and throughout the Midwest. They drew three million fans that year, and the Metrodome was rocking. The Hubert H. Humphrey Metrodome was a miserable place to play baseball—much like Tropicana Field is today—but it served its purpose. The Twins played extremely well there, and they were never rained or snowed out.

After the 1989 season, I got my first national network job. That was as emotional for me as when I was called up to the major leagues in 1959. CBS had acquired the rights to televise baseball games for the next four years. They held auditions for several announcers and former players. Brent Musburger, whom I had first met in Chicago in the early '60s when he was a reporter for the *Chicago American*, was an announcer on CBS who was identified with college football and the NFL pregame show. He also did the College World Series final game. He would come to Omaha, the longtime site of the College World Series, a day or two ahead of time to do the research. I had been announcing those games on ESPN because the Twins allowed me to leave for a few weeks to cover it. Musburger had been very complimentary about me to Ted Shaker, the executive producer of CBS Sports, and told Shaker to be sure to give me a shot at the job.

Joe Morgan; Johnny Bench; and Schmidt, my friend and former teammate, were all auditioning for the job. At the time the national television critic for sports was Rudy Martzke. Network executives practically bowed down to him. Martzke was touting the big names for the job, and my name was never mentioned. Shaker called me and said, "Be patient. I am selling you for the job to Neal Pilson." The president of CBS Sports, Pilson was prone to take the big names.

After doing some audition games with Musburger, Dick Stockton, and Jack Buck, I felt that I did a good job. It was a game changer and a life changer when Shaker called me to say that I had been chosen to work the B game with Buck. The A team would be Musburger and my friend and former teammate, McCarver. Before Opening Day in 1990, Musburger and CBS could not reach a contract agreement, and Musburger was fired the day of the NCAA basketball finals. Buck was moved up to the A team. I would be working with Dick Stockton, who would become a great friend and was very helpful in my further development as an analyst—as was director Joe Aceti.

I worked 16 games a season for CBS for the next four seasons and got to be a sideline reporter and postgame presenter of the World Series trophy. I will never forget when the Reds swept the heavily-favored Oakland A's in the 1990 World Series. I got to present the World Series trophy to Reds manager Lou Piniella and Schott, who had had a few adult beverages during the game. I grabbed her by the back of her jacket and held her like Edgar Bergen held his puppet Charlie McCarthy.

In 1991 the Twins returned to the World Series, and since I was one of their announcers during the season, that was a special thrill for me. I got to interview Kirby Puckett after his famous home run to win Game 6 and then Jack Morris, who pitched one of the great Game 7s in World Series history—a 1–0 10-inning victory. I have never heard such noise as the roar by the fans in the Metrodome. It's amazing how a baseball team can energize a city!

I did two more years at CBS and for the Twins. Then ESPN approached me about being an analyst on their new show called *Baseball Tonight*. I was sad to leave the Twins, but the executives at WCCO, the Twins' flagship station, understood my desire to do national broadcasts.

In January of 1988, MaryAnn Montanaro and I were married by a justice of the peace in Clearwater, Florida, just to be legal. Then in November of that year we had an official wedding in Boca Raton, Florida, with a very enjoyable reception on a 110-foot yacht with the entire wedding party and guests floating up and down the Intracoastal Waterway on a beautiful evening.

Later that year I had the privilege of broadcasting baseball games from the Seoul Olympics on NBC. My partner in the booth was Jay Randolph, a broadcaster for the Cardinals, Reds, and Florida Marlins. His father, Jennings Randolph, was a United States senator from West Virginia. It was interesting to me to see how Seoul had been rebuilt after the Korean War in the 1950s. When I wasn't covering the Olympic baseball competition, I got to see some other Olympic events. I saw Edwin Moses lose the 400-meter high hurdles for the first time and go home with a bronze medal. I saw Canadian Ben Johnson run the fastest 100 meters and win the gold—only to have his medal and victory stripped from him because of steroid use. The gold was later awarded to Carl Lewis.

Baseball was only a demonstration sport in the 1988 Olympics. Because the games are usually held when it's baseball season in the U.S., Major League Baseball has refused to take a break and send America's best players to compete. (By comparison, every four years the NHL takes a break from its season to send its best players to the Winter Olympics.) The USA team included minor leaguers and college players, a number of whom wound up as major leaguers, including Jim Abbott, Robin Ventura, Ed Sprague Jr., Andy Benes, Tino Martinez, Bret Barberie, Jeff Branson, Tom Goodwin, Ben McDonald, Dave Silvestri, Joe Slusarki, Mickey Morandini, Mike Milchin, Charles Nagy, Scott Servais, and Ted Wood. The USA beat Japan 5–3 in the final. It was a coming-out party for future stars and future Yankees in particular. Abbott pitched a complete game, Martinez hit two home runs, and the U.S. won gold.

CHAPTER 5

Broadcasting

As a broadcaster I was fortunate—thanks to Tony Kubek and Don Drysdale—to be able to travel on my own and stay in a different hotel from the ballclub. That's always a good policy in my opinion. I'm not one of the team members. I'm an honest and objective announcer. I always cringed when I would hear an announcer say to me, "We are making too many mistakes on the bases." It's not we! It's the New York Yankees or the Minnesota Twins.

I never spent much time with other broadcasters unless we happened to stay at the same hotel. When I was doing Yankees games in 1986, I stayed at the Regency Hotel in Manhattan. So did Tim McCarver when he was announcing New York Mets games. Once or twice a season, we would be in town at the same time and get together for dinner. My broadcast partners like Ken Singleton, Dick Bremer, and Bob Costas would get together for dinner on occasion, and some of our production team would join us as well.

MaryAnn and I made our winter home in Florida but moved to Madison, Connecticut, for the summer of 1994. It was just an hour's commute from ESPN's studios in Bristol,

Connecticut. It was well worth the commute to live in this beautiful seaside village. I soon found out that my gig on *Baseball Tonight* was more window dressing than in-depth baseball analysis. John Walsh and Steve Anderson were the men who hired me. They made a lunch date to see how I thought things was going for me. I was brutally honest with them. I told them that they were paying me a lot of money to sit on the *Baseball Tonight* set and not say very much. Their philosophy was that they wanted a big league presence on the set while Chris Berman, Chris Myers, or Craig Kilborn went through all the highlights of the day's games. I didn't have to say much. I thought that they could have put a cardboard cutout of me on the set with the host. I understood their reasoning. It was a highlight-driven show. Fans tuned in to see the highlights and find out who won. There was not much analyzing to do. I also did some MLB games as part of my job. I suggested that perhaps I could contribute more if I were at a big league ballpark and made some contribution to the show from the parks.

Then a surprising event changed my life and my career. MaryAnn and I enjoyed rollerblading. The streets on Middle Beach Road in Madison had just been freshly blacktopped—perfect for that exercise. One afternoon as we skated past a house, I heard my name called. "Hey, Kitty!" I knew if they called me Kitty, they knew me. That's a nickname Chuck

Stobbs gave me in 1958. It's a play on those who pronounced my name "Cat" instead of "Cot." I was (at least then) the young cat, the "kitty cat."

So we stopped and went back to see who had called out to me by my nickname. It turned out to be Bryan Burns, who at the time had the title of director of Major League Baseball Broadcasting. He told me that the Madison Square Garden Network was trying to reach me. Kubek was retiring as a Yankees broadcaster and he had recommended me to be his replacement.

I have thanked Kubek many times since then, as being an analyst on the New York Yankees television network is probably the best local television job a former player could have—both in terms of prestige and money. I never took that for granted. I have always been extremely grateful for having that position for 12 years. Doug Moss, the president of the MSG Network, had just left to become president of the Buffalo Sabres NHL franchise. Mike McCarthy was taking over as president of the MSG Network, and Burns suggested that I call him. Burns gave me his number, and I called McCarthy. He was prepared to offer me the job, but he had one problem to overcome: I had a multi-year deal with ESPN and I wanted to handle this properly.

I met with Howard Katz, the executive vice president of broadcasting for ESPN, and told him of my desire to get back to the ballpark, but I would not break my contract with ESPN. They had been more than fair with me, and I was going to do, as I had been raised to do, the right thing. Katz was unbelievably gracious in allowing me to leave. Plus, because no games were being played due to the players' strike, *Baseball Tonight* was shut down for the time being anyway. He still graciously paid out my entire contract for 1994. I was not accustomed to that kind of generosity. So I called McCarthy and said I was free to work for MSG covering the Yankees. To this day—and with no malice or disrespect to other TV executives or networks—MSG and McCarthy were the finest group of people I have ever worked for in the broadcasting business. Marty Brooks, Barry Watkins, Dave Checketts, and McCarthy gave me first-class treatment beyond what I deserved.

Then came an interesting contract negotiation. McCarthy thought I was a client of Ed Hookstratten, a high-powered Los Angeles agent whose clients included Johnny Carson and Pat Riley. He also represented Dick Stockton and his wife, Leslie Visser. Hook had been a pitcher in college—a lefty—and and had wanted to represent me in 1993. I agreed. I was in the process of reupping with the Minnesota Twins Network before the ESPN offer came along. John Cullerton was the president and a first-class young man. Hook sent them a vulgar reply to their first offer. I had not signed an agreement with Hook yet. I called him and said, "Let's call this off right now. I don't approve of doing business the way you responded to WCCO." We mutually agreed to part ways before we really started.

Meanwhile, McCarthy thought I was represented by Hookstratten, and said to me, "I guess I call Ed Hookstratten to work out a contract."

My late wife, MaryAnn, was a savvy businesswoman and thought she could handle my contract negotiations. She could and she did. I told McCarthy, "No, I'm represented by MaryAnn Montanaro."

Then Kubek called and volunteered to give me the details of his contract. MaryAnn had all the notes from that conversation. It wasn't a difficult negotiation. McCarthy laughed about it later and said, "I wish you would have still been represented by Hookstratten!" MaryAnn negotiated every MSG and YES contract I signed. Sandy Montag, a first-class gentleman, has been handling my contracts with the MLB Network, and that has also been easy. Montag represents Costas, John Madden, and many people in the television business. Tony Petitti and now Rob McGlarry, the CEOs of the MLB Network, have been very fair to me, and I am fortunate to be doing a little work at age 83. It allows me to stay connected to the game I have been passionate about since the mid-1940s.

Anyhow, once my contract got situated with the Yankees broadcast, my partner for the first two years was Dave Cohen, a New York city native with a big voice and a love of baseball. After two years, MSG decided to use two former players who could do play-by-play as well as color analysis. In 1997 MSG auditioned several different former players, but it was apparent to me that the best fit would be Ken Singleton. Singy had been a major leaguer for 15 years with the Mets, Montreal Expos, and Baltimore Orioles. He was familiar with the Yankees and he had done play-by-play for the Expos on the Montreal network. I showed the demo disc of all the different partners I had tried out with and asked MaryAnn whom she felt was the best fit for me. After watching the videos, she also thought Singleton. MSG felt the same way.

Singleton and I were a two-man team for six seasons, and those were the easiest and smoothest telecasts of my career. No disrespect to any of my other partners, but two former players, who can each do play-by-play, are like two friends attending the games as spectators and just talkin' baseball. And we were talking about what was happening on the field with a combination of almost 45 years of major league playing experience.

I have always been humbled to think of how a country kid from the Midwest was accepted by the passionate fans of the Yankees. I am still pleased when Yankees fans stop and mention how much they enjoyed our telecasts. We had a great production team: Leon Schweir was our producer. Bill Webb, an Emmy Award-winning director, and John Moon directed. Many of our production team staffers—whether they were camera operators or in the production truck—are still working baseball on national networks.

I had many highlights during my years covering the Yankees. David Wells' perfect game on May 17, 1998—against the Twins, my former team—stands out. I have learned that broadcasters should keep fans informed that a pitcher has a no-hitter going. I failed to do that when I announced Doc Gooden's no-hitter on May 14, 1996, and the television writers were critical of me for not saying anything on the air. They were and are right. Keep fans updated. Not mentioning a no-hitter if you are *sitting on the dugout bench* is a different matter.

It's so hard to single out one player as the biggest reason for the Yankees' success, but I felt that every year they won it all, Mariano Rivera was always their Most Valuable Player. Put him on Atlanta Braves teams in the 1990s, and they probably would have won several World Series. In 2019 Rivera became the first man ever inducted into the Baseball Hall of Fame by a unanimous vote of the writers. It was a well-deserved honor.

Another highlight of my Yankee years was the July 1, 2004, game in which Yankees shortstop—and now Hall of

Famer—Derek Jeter dove into the stands for a foul ball and bloodied his face. In the same game, Nomar Garciaparra of the Boston Red Sox caused a stir as to why he wasn't standing up with all of his teammates. There are many stories about why Garciaparra couldn't play that day and why he sat on the bench the whole game. Only he knows why. Whatever the reason, it did not cast him in a good light in an important game like that. The Red Sox traded him on July 31 that season to the Chicago Cubs, and it helped land them Orlando Cabrera, who contributed to the Red Sox winning the World Series that year.

I also had a thrill broadcasting Jeter's final game on September 28, 2014, with Costas on MLB Network. That was really special. Covering the 1998 Yankees for the entire season was as good as an announcer could experience. It was the best all-around team since maybe the 1984 Detroit Tigers. They could do everything well. They had a good starting rotation, a deep bullpen, enough power, savvy baserunners, and great strike-two-hitters who could hit sacrifice flies and opposite-field singles.

But announcing the Yankees had its obvious challenges, too. When the Yankees acquired Charlie Hayes from the Pittsburgh Pirates to play third base the last part of the '96 season, Jim Leyritz and Wade Boggs voiced their displeasure. I'm sure it was just a natural knee-jerk reaction. Leyritz said,

My favorite piece of memorabilia is the photograph of my dad and I standing on the field of Metropolitan Stadium in Bloomington, Minnesota, prior to Game 7 of the 1965 World Series.

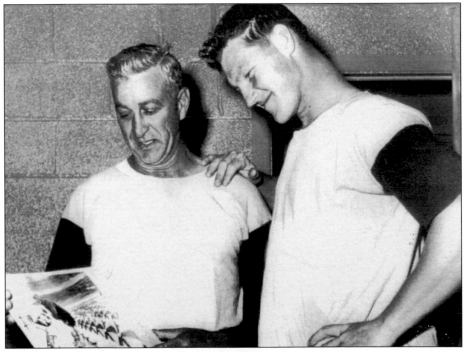

I stand next to Sam Mele, my former Minnesota Twins manager.

This is the home I grew up in at 44 Wall Street in Zeeland, Michigan.

My hometown did a great job of rooting me on during the 1965 World Series.

I pitched alongside Hall of Famer Rich "Goose" Gossage from 1973 to 1975 with the Chicago White Sox.

While coaching the Cincinnati Reds under Pete Rose, I hang out with pitching great Nolan Ryan prior to a game in the 1980s.

I saved an edition of *The Sporting News* from 1974 because it's a great picture of me standing next to several of the 16 Gold Gloves I was awarded.

I stand next to my idol, pitcher Bobby Shantz, who won eight consecutive Gold Gloves, at the presentation of the 2019 Gold Glove Awards.

During my first major league start in 1959, I pitched to Hall of Famer Ted Williams. We became friendly, and I attend a formal function with him in 1996.

I hang out with my good friend Sandy Koufax, whom I faced in the 1965 World Series.

I hang out with two fellow members of the Philadelphia Phillies fraternity—Hall of Famers Richie Ashburn and Steve Carlton—in 1995.

My buddy Mike Schmidt was one of the all-time greatest third basemen.

After joining the Chicago White Sox, I immediately bonded with Dick Allen, who became a lifelong friend.

Whitey Ford and I became friends when I pitched for the New York Yankees, and we met in spring training. We continued that friendship through golf for many decades after that.

One of the best nights I've ever had was when Bill White, Sandy Koufax, Bob Gibson, Tim McCarver, and I had dinner in Florida. Tim and I still recount the great stories that were shared that evening.

A great player and broadcaster, Bill White was a mentor to me and guided me on how to approach calling New York Yankees games.

For the MSG and YES networks, Ken Singleton and I shared play-by-play and analyst duties for six years as a two-man booth. He was a great partner.

I celebrate Jim Kaat Day in May 1991 with loved ones.

My parents and siblings celebrate Thanksgiving in 1977.

I hang out with grandsons Tanner, Casey, and Brendan in Ridgewood, New Jersey, in 2007.

I chat with longtime player and coach Chili Davis before a 2012 playoff game. *(MLB Network)*

Bob Costas and I announce a game in 2019. Working with Bob for MLB Network has been an absolute pleasure. *(MLB Network)*

"Wade and I can handle third base just fine." And Boggs said, "I guess I'll have to go somewhere else to get my 3,000th hit." (His combined Red Sox/Yankees hits were 2,800.)

We had a section of our telecast sponsored by Budweiser beer. I reacted to Leyritz's comment by saying. "If he thinks he can play third base as well as Charlie Hayes, then he hasn't seen Charlie play third base."

The next day in Oakland, Leyritz rushed up to me and said, "My dad said you ripped me on TV last night."

I said casually, "What did your dad say that I said?" Leyritz responded: "He said, 'you said that I can't play third base.'"

I told him, "Jim, you better go back and look at a tape of the game and come back and tell me exactly what I said."

He later understood what I said. It was a classic example of accuracy altered as information is passed on secondhand. Leyritz and I have a good relationship today. A few years ago, we sat next to each other at The Masters.

When I would see Alex Rodriguez around the batting cage, I would greet him either as "Alex" or as "ARod." At the time he was not doing well late in the games with runners on base and a chance to get an important hit. Teams started stockpiling their hard thrower to use late in the game and they were throwing the fastball right by him. His swing was too long to catch up. Jeter, on the other hand, was getting important hits late in the game. We did a split screen on their respective swings and their late-game production numbers. Rodriguez was hitting close to .150 with men on base. I pointed out that Yankees hitting coach Don Mattingly hesitated to make a change because Rodriguez had obviously been a productive player and he didn't want to rush in and make changes in his first year as a Yankees player.

So the next day after the split screen, I saw Rodriguez and gave him my customary, "Hi, Alex." There was a quick turn away from me and no acknowledgment. I like a challenge, so I waited until I was near him again and said another, "Hi, Alex." Same reaction. No problem. I have plenty of guys I can talk to and don't need him exclusively. It was silent between us the rest of the year.

The next spring Rick Cerrone, the Yankees public relations man, told me that Rodriguez wanted to talk to me. I sought him out in the Yankees' clubhouse. He said he'd like to speak with me in private. So we went into the laundry room in the back of the clubhouse—quite a setting for a high-level meeting. He proceeded to tell me that the previous year had been his first as a Yankee and he had a lot on his plate and probably overreacted and wanted to know if we could start over. I said, "Absolutely. But just let me tell you what my job is as an analyst: to be honest and objective. If you hit 50 home runs and drove in 200 and the Yankees weren't 162–0, my job would be easy. But I'm not your PR man. I work for the viewers and I owe it to them to tell them what I see."

We have been fine ever since, though I don't think it's right that he gets all the exposure he does on TV and was even a candidate to buy the Mets. If I was commissioner, he would have been banned for life after his second offense. He is a well-mannered but insecure individual who seems to crave attention.

In 2003 the Yankees played an interleague series in Cincinnati, the home of Yankees bench coach Don Zimmer, a former legend at Cincinnati's Western Hills High School. A week before the series, there was an organizational dustup when the Yankees had lost 12 of their previous 20 games, and Joe Torre's job as manager was being questioned. Zim's comments were: "When the Yankees are winning, it's the geniuses in Tampa [headquarters of the Yankee minor league operation.] When they lose, it's always Joe Torre's fault."

This did not please John Filipelli, executive producer of YES. One of our stock shots on TV was to show Torre and Zim seated side by side the entire game. It portrayed a lot of different emotions—mostly laughing and enjoying the Yankees' success. I got a call from Kevin Smolen, our producer of the YES games, alerting me that we were not to show that shot during the Cincinnati series per George Steinbrenner's orders. We weren't even going to show Zim. I had to think about that before reacting. I decided to call our founder and CEO, Leo Hindery, and ask Hindery if I could take a leave of absence for those three games. I could not announce three Yankees games in Cincinnati without mentioning or showing Zim. Torre already told Zim he could take the lineup cards to home plate every game. Hindery understood my dilemma and said, "You go to Cincinnati and you talk about Zim all you want."

Obviously Filipelli was not pleased. But the issue was a recurring theme with Flip. Word must have reached Zim about what I did. A week or so after we returned from Cincinnati, he called me over and emotionally thanked me for what I had done because getting some love from Cincinnati fans was a big deal to him.

It turns out that Steinbrenner never said anything about not showing Zim. Flip had a habit of preempting what he *thought* Steinbrenner's reaction might be to Zim's remarks. I would occasionally be on the office elevator with Steinbrenner after a game and I would be open about things I had said that annoyed him. His answer was: "I'm never upset with you, Jim. You tell it like it is. I wish everybody did."

The second item that further caused a divide between Flip and me was our nightly "Player of the Game" announcement. Tanyon Sturtze, one of the Yankees relievers, had come in and pitched a few very effective innings to impact a Yankees win.

In the eighth inning, Schweir, our producer, usually asked, "Kitty, who is your player of the game?" Sturtze was the no-brainer choice. So the guys in the truck built a little highlight package of what he did. In the bottom of the eighth, Gary Sheffield hit a solo home run in a blowout situation. It had no impact on the game. Schweir said to me on the talkback line: "I got a call, and Flip wants us to name Sheffield as the player of the game. He said it would please George because George was a big fan of Sheffield."

No offense to the talented Sheffield, but anybody watching that game knew that Sturtze had more of an impact on the game than Sheffield. Schweir was in a tough spot. I said, "Go ahead and build your Sheffield piece, and I'll handle it." The way I handled it was to say: "Those of you who watched tonight's game know that Tanyon Sturtze was the Yankee player of the game, but at the last minute, someone stuffed the ballot box and changed it to Gary Sheffield." And then we showed Sheffield's home run.

It was an example of what Bill White had taught me years ago of not compromising my credibility. Some may see it as insubordination, but if an analyst is hired to analyze a game, he should be allowed to do that. If it's a legal matter or a sensitive issue the network wishes to stay clear of, they should not put words in our mouth. Filipelli is the only executive producer who ever did that to me.

For the MSG and YES networks, Singleton and I shared play-by-play and analyst duties for six years as a two-man booth. Former players are usually analysts when they transition to the broadcast booth. My mentor White, who played mostly first base for the San Francisco Giants, St. Louis Cardinals, and the Philadelphia Phillies in 1956 and 1958–69, did both play-by-play and analysis for Yankees games for 18 years. From 1989 to 1994, he was the president of the National League. White suggested that I take a recorder to spring training games and practice play-by-play calls. He said, "It gives you an extra dimension to offer to networks." That advice has served me well.

The fundamental difference is that the play-by-play person does the who and where. *Who is the player? Where is he from? What is his background?* He or she may add some interesting stories about the player. The analyst does the how and why, describing how he made that play or pitch or why the manager did a certain thing. The pure play-by-play person is more important on a national game, where the players may be unknown to a national audience. The viewer may not have seen this team and this player before. When you do 100 games a year for one team and have most of the same fans game after game, that is not as important. It is actually easier to do games covering one team because you have game after game to refer back to and can talk about what has happened with a team or player and what is happening now.

I have had some elite partners as play-by-play specialists, including Dick Enberg, Stockton, Greg Gumbel, Sean McDonough, and Jay Randolph. My other terrific broadcasting partners were: Kenny Albert, George Grande, Costas, White, Buck Showalter, Phil Rizzuto, George Frazier, Bremer, Ted Robinson, Billy Martin, Al Trautwig, Cohen, David Cone, Singleton, Suzyn Waldman, Michael Kay, Bobby Murcer, Paul O'Neill, Joe Girardi, David Justice, Al Leiter, John Flaherty, Tom Verducci, John Smoltz, Ralph Kiner, Warner Fusselle, Phil Stone, Jim Nantz, Don Orsillo, Joe Buck, Sam Rosen, John Sanders, Matt Vasgersian, Paul Severino, Rich Waltz, Chris German, Herb Carneal, Skip Caray, Ernie Johnson, Pete van Wieren, Chip Caray, Steve Stone, Richie Ashburn, and Gary Thorne.

My current broadcast partner, Costas, is as versatile and talented an announcer as there is in the business. What makes working with him so easy and enjoyable is that we have become close friends, having been a team for 11 years. Bremer and I have the same friendly relationship and have done Twins games on their network for several years.

In recent years networks have added nationally-known writers who do sideline reporting on interesting things they have dug up behind the scenes. Sometimes, though, it can create some controversy if the sideline reporter slides over and starts analyzing what is going on in the game. That's dangerous when they're working with a former player. Unless they have been between the lines and competed in a major league game, they have no right trying to make it sound like they actually know what the players know any more than I know what it is like to write articles.

When I first started analyzing games on television, I was so concerned, as many still are I'm sure, that I was going to need a lot of material to fill up two-and-a-half hours of time. Now it's more than three and sometimes four. I seldom used all my material, but sometimes I jammed a note I had written down into a pocket and then later thought, *That really didn't need to be said*. I was doing CBS telecasts on Saturday afternoons in addition to my Twins telecasts from 1990 to 1993. WCCO-TV carried 30 Twins games on their network and the station wanted me to make every effort to do all of those games.

Those CBS games were available to the public. You didn't need a cable subscription. So I did an afternoon game at Wrigley Field, had a driver hustle me to O'Hare Airport, caught a late afternoon flight to Minneapolis, and had a driver meet me and hustle me to the Metrodome for the 7:00 PM Twins' game that night. I walked into the booth as the national anthem was being sung. There was no time for notes. I had a scorecard and that was it. My play-by-play partner at the time was Robinson. He did all the nuts-and-bolts stuff, which play-by-play announcers do, and I just watched the game and commented on what I saw. I never felt more comfortable analyzing a game or was more into a game.

I called my CBS partner Stockton the next day as we usually talked about our game the day before and did some self-critiquing. I told him of my experience the night before. He said, "Madden doesn't have notes."

"Really? Would he talk to me about that?" I asked.

Stockton arranged the call because he and Madden had called some football games together. Madden was so gracious. He was an avid baseball fan. He explained that he did his homework and wanted to be sure he was accurate with pronunciations and the personality and skills of a player, tendencies of coaches, etc. And then he just watched the game. What a concept! I have not used many notes and sometimes none at all since our conversations. I'm sure some of my partners have looked at the counter in front of me in the booth and wondered. *Where are his notes?* Yes, I write down a particular important point that I don't want to forget, but as Madden told me, "If you have things written down, you have a tendency to get them in even if they might not pertain to the game at that moment. If you forget something, it probably wasn't that important anyway." That advice has served me well in analyzing games for years.

What is my homework? Before a game I receive a lot of printed notes, which each team provides to our MLB Network research team. While covering the Yankees, we got the game notes in the broadcast booth well before the game. I cherry pick those and try to memorize the important facts. Is this the pitcher's major league debut? If he gets a win, does he reach some milestone like his 100th win?

We usually have some time with the team managers about three hours prior to game time. I like to speak with the pitching coaches. I know most of them well. I try to get a little information on that night's starter: his recent form, anything new that he is doing differently. I also want to find out who is unavailable in the bullpen, who is apt to be your sixth-inning option, which position players are available off the bench. If I have a question about the correct pronunciation of a player's name, I check with the media relations rep.

Then I try to watch a little batting practice. I might find a player to speak with about something. Team broadcasters—like Yankees broadcaster Cone—usually have pertinent information. I check out the field conditions. Did it just rain? Is the wind a factor? If I have a specific question, which I wish to ask a manager or coach, I'll find him when he's alone and sneak it in. I have the advantage of knowing most of them, and they trust that I am not going to break a confidence. If it's something of a sensitive nature, I'll figure out a way to phrase it. I might say, "It looks to me like Joe Smith has changed his stance since we last saw him" or "The Braves' catcher is moving too early before the pitch. I think the coaches might be working with him on correcting that."

After MaryAnn was diagnosed with bladder cancer in 2004, I cut back to just about 50 games a season, mostly in New York or the eastern cities. As MaryAnn's health deteriorated, I knew I was going to have to stop announcing and devote all my time to her as a caregiver.

I gave YES notice that 2006 would be my last year. Steinbrenner had Debbie Tymon, the Yankees marketing director, tell me that he wanted me to throw out the ceremonial first pitch before my last game. It was in mid-September, and I was scheduled to work the game with Murcer. But the game was rained out, and I threw out the first pitch on Saturday. Tymon let me take three of my grandchildren to the mound with me to help me throw the pitch. It was extra special to have my grandchildren, Brendan, Tanner, and Casey there on the Saturday afternoon game. Steinbrenner had arranged for YES to do a video with Singleton voicing it. It was a nationally televised game, and my friend, McCarver, was one of the announcers and invited me to visit the booth for an inning.

After my time at YES, my friend Russ Gabay, who was a runner and then a producer for ESPN when I did college baseball for them in the mid-1980s, had become the executive producer of Baseball International. They call it a runner because they would often run to get a cup of coffee for the sportscaster, but Gabay impressively rose from that position through hard work. Anyhow, he called and asked if I was interested in working a little again. He offered me the analyst job on the World Baseball Classic pool, which took place in March in Puerto Rico. I took that gig and loved announcing it with Waltz. I have worked the WBC games ever since then. They happen every four years and were postponed in 2021 because of Covid-19 and will take place in 2022. I will be 83 then. I'd love to do them!

In January of 2009, the MLB Network was formed. Petitti was hired as the CEO and put the entire network together. He called and asked if I'd like to do some MLB games. I asked how many games he had in mind because I didn't know if I wanted to do a full slate of 50 to 75 games. He asked how many I would like to do and I half-kidding told him 10. He said, "Perfect! I want to pair you with Bob Costas, and with all of his NBC commitments, that is about the number he could do."

That was great news. Costas and I had known each other for years but never worked together. We have become good friends, and I think that is an advantage in doing our games. We both have great respect for the game and a knowledge of its history. Costas opted not to do games in 2020, and I am happy that we did some games again in 2021.

Being on a team that produces baseball games is a little like being on a baseball team. There are a lot of people down in the production truck who are responsible for getting a game on the air. It starts with our producer, Chris Pfeiffer, who produced the WBC games I did as well. Directors John Moore and Jason Loeb and a host of people are responsible for a variety of tasks in the truck. Many people, whom the viewer doesn't see, are very important to producing a good telecast: producers, directors, research and statistical support people, stage managers, countless technicians, and camera operators. A big thanks to all of you who made my job go smoothly and efficiently. Doing games in 2020 meant my MLB career has touched eight decades as a player, a coach, and a broadcaster. I don't know how many others have been involved that many years. I'm sure it's a small number. I have been very fortunate.

When I started announcing games, many were college games I did on ESPN with Rosen, who was better known as the "voice of the New York Rangers." Rosen made me feel so comfortable in the booth. Fred Gaudelli, who has become a star as the producer of *Sunday Night Football* on NBC, was one of the producers for baseball games on ESPN in the mid-1980s. Gaudelli invited me to sit in the production truck on games I wasn't working and get an idea of how busy and often chaotic it can be in there. There is a button called the talkback button, which the announcers can use to speak to the producer without being heard over the air. Gaudelli took the time to show me how and when to use that. What a great help to me that has been.

Bob Dekas and Bob Fishman were the producer and director, respectively, for games I broadcast for CBS for four years. They showed me how a national network game is done. It's a little different than local games. Fish is still widely acclaimed as a director of NFL games and has directed the Final Four for decades as well as the Daytona 500.

When I did Yankees games on the Madison Square Garden Network for seven years, we really were a team, doing as many as 75 home games a season. In addition to Singleton and Schweir, we also had Trautwig as host, and our Emmy Award-winning director was the legendary Bill Webb. Mike Scheinkman was as good a research and stat man you could find on Yankees baseball. He was by my side in the booth. Audrey De Wys was our stage manager and continued that position when YES began producing Yankees games. Aud kept things loose and lighthearted. Doing baseball games on television could never be better than those seven years. McCarthy, our boss, never interfered. I always felt free to speak my mind at MSG, which was not always easy to do with Steinbrenner watching every game. I ended up developing an extremely good working relationship with Steinbrenner despite the disagreements we had when I was playing for him. I announced Yankees games for five more years on the YES Network.

Kay became the play-by-play man with Singleton and me. We worked well together. Kay became a good friend, as most broadcast colleagues do when you do that many games together. He's a former a postgame reporter and a writer who went into the TV booth and has become a star in the New York market. Aud was still there as stage manager, Smolen produced, and Moore directed. I have great memories of my times with all of those people. Announcing games on the Yankees' network is the best local television job in the marketplace, and I never took it for granted. I felt a sense of gratitude every day I was able to be in "The House that Ruth Built." I have announced more than a thousand games at Yankee Stadium, and the people I mentioned above made it easy and enjoyable for me.

The next baseball game you watch, I hope you will think of all the people behind the scenes that make us look better and sound smarter than we really are. As the great Jack Buck told me back in 1983 when we crossed paths in Philadelphia while covering the World Series: "I heard you are getting into this TV business."

I said, "Well, I'm trying it out to see if I can do it."

He called me over to a quiet corner. I was expecting some sage advice. He whispered, "Don't tell people how easy it *is*. Just smile and cash the checks."

It is easy. I often call it "legal robbery" and I am so grateful for the gift of being able to do it and for the people who help me do it!

CHAPTER 6

My Likes and Dislikes

There are many things that attracted me to Major League Baseball, but now there are certain aspects that are less appealing. I like the athletic ability of the pitchers and players. It has never been better. I use my own ability as a measuring stick. I began to see it when I was announcing New York Yankees games in the mid 1990s and I saw Andy Pettitte use pitches at age 22 that I couldn't use at that age. He had better control of a curve, added a cutter, was more consistent than I was. Then I began to see it in the ability of the position players. The athleticism of the players is exceptional, and it just keeps getting better. Center field and shortstop are probably the most telling positions of improvement. A lot of them play it like Willie Mays, who stood out because there was only one Mays.

Many have commented to me over the years: "I bet you wish you were playing today. Think of the money you'd be making." Of course, they are right about the money. A player can be a free agent after six full seasons in the big leagues. For me that would have been after the 1966 season. I would've been 28 years old. 1964, '65, and '66 were seasons which certainly would put me in the Gerrit Cole/Justin Verlander salary bracket. I don't think it is a stretch to say that I would have become the highest-paid pitcher in the American League. By today's standards, I'd probably have signed a long-term deal for about $30 million per year. I was paid a little more $2 million dollars over my 25 major league contracts, topping out at $285,000 in 1983. I thought I was really overpaid during my last season when I was a part-time pitcher but had a big-time salary.

The one thing I would have enjoyed, which today's money would have enabled, was to fly on private planes. But I also would have loved to have played in the era right after the players came back from World War II. There were just 16 teams. You played each team 22 times and traveled by train. I love train travel. That was baseball's golden era for me: 1946-1957. When the Dodgers moved to Los Angeles and the Giants moved to San Francisco in 1958, Western civilization began to go downhill. Not really. That's just the voice of an old dinosaur who loved the hit-and-run, leadoff triples, squeeze plays, and pitchers who could field their positions like Bobby Shantz.

I liked to read the box scores the day after the Yankees played the Cleveland Indians in a doubleheader and Vic Raschi "The Springfield Rifle," Allie Reynolds "Superchief," "Rapid" Robert Feller, Bob Lemon, and Early Wynn all pitched complete games. It was two-and-a-half hours of good entertainment with some action. That's all it should take for an exciting baseball game unless, of course, it's the 16-inning epic battle in 1963 when Mays hit a home run off Warren Spahn to win it. I'm sure a lot of fans left. I don't think I would have left. That kind of game is not popular anymore.

You could count on the same lineups on most of the teams for many years. I had most of them memorized. I think of my friend, John Ortberg, who is a pastor on the West Coast, asking another pastor, David Hubbard, if he could name the starting lineup of Hubbard's beloved Dodgers back in the '50s. Hubbard named them all and asked Ortberg, "Would you like me to tell you the starting lineups for *all* the teams?" That's how passionate we were about our teams. My team was the Philadelphia Athletics, who had Shantz, my boyhood hero, on their staff.

I was fortunate to be a member of an exciting team in 1982—the St. Louis Cardinals. We won the World Series. We hit 67 home runs as a team but stole 200 bases. That team was as much fun to watch as it was to play for. The 1991 Minnesota Twins team was exciting as well. The 1998 New York Yankees, too. But suddenly the game began to slip into a game of who can hit the most home runs. Build and conform your ballpark so everybody can hit one out of the park. Marketing the game seemed to become more important than staying true to how the game was designed to be an American Pastime for years. And now in 2021, the game is talked about as how enjoyable it was to watch at one time but how unwatchable it can be today. I even have executives and current personnel tell me, "Boy, it's a different game than the one you played." No, it's *not* a different game. But it is operated and managed differently.

Televising games has been great for the game. Many owners thought that when more games were televised, particularly on so-called "free TV," people would stop coming to the ballpark. In fact, the opposite is true. Televising baseball games has created fans because it gets them engrossed in the product. I am grateful for being able to broadcast baseball games. From following the game since I was seven in 1945, playing professionally for 27 years, then coaching, and seeing it from the TV broadcast booth for the past 35 years, I have developed strong opinions on the game and things I don't think are making it as appealing as it once was.

There are plenty of things I like about today's game, including the athleticism of the players. The modern players can do things that no previous eras' players could. It's the most attractive thing about today's game of baseball. I love watching Javier Báez turn the double play or Jackie Bradley Jr. track fly balls. I'm happy whenever the Dodgers catcher Will Smith gets a big hit. He has no chains, beard, or visible tattoos. He's my kind of young man. I love watching Nolan Arenado make plays at third base. I love watching Mike Trout and Christian Yelich hit. I love watching elite pitchers pitch. I loved watching Ichiro Suzuiki play. He could hit, run, and throw. Hideki Matsui could too. Each was the epitome of professionalism in his conduct and play. They had high baseball IQs.

Now there are some things I dislike in today's game when compared to the game I knew in my youth and playing days. I don't like the contact rules on sliding into second base or home plate. I think it's sad that teams don't take infield practice where fans can see them. That's part of the fun of actually going to the ballpark and getting there early. I dislike catchers who move too much and too early before the pitch is thrown. Catchers are trained to wait until the last second to shift laterally to where they would like the pitch thrown. If they move too early, batters can sense where the pitch might be thrown. With the inexperience of young pitchers and the modern emphasis on velocity over control, catchers would be better off setting up with their entire body behind the plate.

I liked the original Yankee Stadium, which existed from 1923 to 1973. I think editions No. 2 (after the 1974–1975 renovations) and No. 3 (the new Yankee Stadium, which opened in 2009) are progressively less attractive than the original. Public-address announcer Bob Sheppard's voice sounded so much better when the speakers were at field level. Of the current stadiums, Camden Yards in Baltimore is the only one with ballpark charm.

Yankee Stadium III opened on April 16, 2009 with a home-opener game against the Cleveland Indians before 48,271 fans. The Yankees decided to use a player whose name started with each letter of the alphabet to form a semicircle from foul line to foul line right behind the infield. Because K is the 11th letter, I was positioned directly behind second base between two very famous Yankees: Reggie Jackson and Don Larsen. I didn't get to meet or visit with all of the players there because the MLB Network was televising the game and I was one of their announcers. I had to do some pregame announcing in the broadcast booth, get downstairs for the opening ceremony, and then quickly back up to the booth for the start of the game. I did get to visit a little with Luis Arroyo, the former Yankees reliever. It was a nice ceremony, but I still preferred the layout of the original Yankee Stadium.

I don't like the blaring sound systems at modern stadiums, and walk-up music, which is not spontaneous, seems self-centered and arrogant. When Hank Blalock of the Texas Rangers was asked what he wanted as his walk-up music, he answered, "Walk-up music? I'm not going up there to *dance*. I'm going up to *hit*."

Some walk-up music isn't played because a player has asked for it but because the organist thought it appropriate. When Dick Allen was having an MVP year in 1972 with the Chicago White Sox, Comiskey Park organist Nancy Faust decided to play "Jesus Christ Superstar" when Allen came up to bat. He homered, and the song stuck. If you asked Allen what song he wanted for walk-up music, I'll promise you that he'd turn around and walk away without answering. The only walk-up music I enjoyed was Metallica's "Enter Sandman," which was played at Yankee Stadium when Mariano Rivera came into the game. Rivera never asked for "Enter Sandman," but it became the most famous walk-up music in the game.

There are not enough complete games these days. I know modern baseball writers, particularly Keith Law of The Athletic, say that we what we did—in terms of complete games—was "a bag of hair" in his words. The win and the complete game are dead. As Del Wilber, my manager with the Triple A Charleston Senators, told me, "We can find a lot of pitchers who can pitch losing games, but it's hard to find the ones who can go the distance and win." The analytics geniuses like Law and Brian Kenny don't understand that. Most managers would prefer to let their starter roll when he has his A game, but they are hesitant because of analytics. It's interesting to see what pitchers' records are when they go the distance. In my 180 complete games, my won-loss record was 146–33 plus one tie from a suspended game in 1967. My ERA for those games was 1.52.

Baseball lived a long and happy life before the invention of the radar gun. We know Walter Johnson was fast—probably the fastest pitcher. The same goes for Feller, Ryne Duren, Nolan Ryan, "Sudden" Sam McDowell, Goose Gossage, and Steve Dalkowski, who, despite his overwhelming speed, never made it to the majors. (He had no control.) What's the difference if their fastballs were 103 mph or 97? The game was the thing.

The radar gun was invented by John L. Barker Sr. and Ben Midlock in Norwalk, Connecticut, during World War II for military use. Today, it has two main uses: to track speeders on the highway and to measure the speed of a pitcher's fastball. That information may be useful to scouts and to the front office. But having the speed flashed on a message board at the ballpark is just a distraction. It takes away from watching the game. Even worse, in my view, is when the speed of the previous pitch is flashed on your TV screen at home. What are you supposed to look at: the action on the field or that number?

Bob Bowman, the CEO of MLBAM (Major League Baseball Advanced Media), made a lot of money for the team owners by creating MLBAM. A few years ago, MLB sold it to Disney for more than $1.5 billion, and each team owner got a nice $30 million windfall. BAM, as they called it, created Statcast, which measures launch angle, exit velocity, ground covered by the fielder in seconds and fractions, radar gun readings—all sorts of data. As my friend and former teammate Jim Beattie, a general manager for a few teams, told me, "That stuff belongs in the offices of teams, not on the TV screen."

Theo Epstein agrees. After leaving his position as general manager of the Chicago Cubs after the 2020 season, he said, "What I did using analytics was helpful building a team and maybe using them in games, but it took away from the aesthetic aspect of the game, the art and skill of the players."

When MLBAM wanted to show Statcast to the MLB Network people in the winter of 2015, a seminar was scheduled and all of us on-air people were required to be there in Secaucus, New Jersey. I'll never forget that meeting. Everyone seemed gaga over what it was going to do to change the way we look at the game, evaluate players, and tailor our TV production. On the flight back to Florida that day, I said to myself, *It will change the game all right, but not for the better.*

Along with the radar gun, Statcast—despite being a revenue producer for the owners—is one of the worst things to happen to the attractiveness of baseball in my lifetime. It has given talking heads, who never played the game, a chance a to spew out metrics and stats that make it sound like they actually know what it's like to be between the lines playing the game. They are unable to realize that players don't feel the same every day—nor do they perform exactly the same way every day. Even uniformed personnel remark to me consistently how the game is being run by the "people upstairs." They don't like it, but many have jobs that pay them good money and they are getting years of service in the MLB pension plan.

In the field of metrics, sabermetrics, analytics—anything you want to call it—I found a woman, Merrianna McCully, who was way ahead of the curve. I was announcing Twins games in the late '80s when I received a letter—not an email or text but a real handwritten letter—about my comments on pitching. McCully lives in the Seattle area and is a huge Mariners fan. Her letter said that she thought I knew more about the Mariners pitchers than the local announcers. It was very flattering. She got my attention. She sent me a graph of how she tracks pitchers' effectiveness. I used the statistics she provided me for over 20 years, and CBS hired her to give me support for the games I did for the network. MSG Network did, too. I have used her rule for years: the goal of every game is to score at least four and allow three or fewer runs. Most games are decided with that metric and have been since the start of the 20th century. She has written that baseball is a game of statistics and percentages, and the only statistic that matters is: "At the end of the game if your team has scored at least one more run than the opposition, your percentage of winning is 100 percent." I like that stat. It's easy to follow, succinct, and 100 percent true.

Oh, how I wish those analytic people would have been working for the Los Angeles Dodgers in Game Seven of the 1965 World Series! We had a couple of men on base, and Sandy Koufax was going through the batting order for the third time. He worked out of the jam and shut us out 2–0. That was the last seven-game World Series where every win was a complete-game win.

Statcast is a distraction. It's counterproductive to enjoyable baseball. Pete Rose, Rod Carew, and Tony Gwynn would not have had great numbers in any of those categories. These sabermetric statistics are causing hitters (except Will Smith) to overswing on every pitch. Pitchers trying to avoid contact leads to long stretches of time when a ball is not put in play. The analytics people have made baseball a very boring game. And on the TV production side, screens are often filled with graphics that are really not pertinent or interesting. The stats aren't even up long enough to read and understand, but our eyes are directed to them, and we take our eyes off the real attractions: the players. Analytics and all the attention our MLB telecasts dedicated to them—mainly the increased use of Statcast elements like launch angle, exit velocity, and pitchers' perceived velocity—is distracting and perhaps confusing for the viewer.

I prefer to talk about things that are happening on the field and the art/skill which the players display—not the science behind it. That's just my opinion. I'm sure there is a certain demographic that likes it. I feel all the unnecessary graphics and things like Statcast force announcers to announce like they're reading the news and not talkin' baseball. When I watch golf or football on television, I want to hear the analysts talk about what the players are thinking and how they are doing what they do. I don't care about all the tendencies and percentages. I still love talking about how baseball players play the game.

I think an example of the analytics obsession is when Kevin Cash, manager of the Tampa Bay Rays, lifted Blake Snell in Game Six of the 2020 World Series because he would be facing Mookie Betts and the Dodgers lineup for the third time. The analytics people have numbers that say that's the time to make a change. What they didn't factor in was that Snell was pitching like he was the current-day Koufax. He was as sharp as he had been all year. And it backfired on Tampa Bay. Cash was second-guessed and criticized for that move. The names of the people in the analytics department should have been exposed. What would the owners and general manager of the Rays have done if Cash had stayed with Snell and the Dodgers scored some runs off him? Would they have fired him? My point is that a manager had to let people with no feel for this particular game influence him to make a decision. Without the influence of the people upstairs, he probably would have stayed with Snell.

It was embarrassing for the Yankees in Game Two of the 2020 American League Division Series when their analytics people thought it would be a good idea to start young Deivi Garcia to get Tampa Bay to have all their left-handed hitters in their lineup and then bring in lefty J.A. Happ in the second inning. That ploy didn't work out well. The Yankees of Ruth, Joe D, Mickey, and Jeter turned to analytics to win a postseason game—and against the team which virtually *invented* the use of an opener. So sad. Postseason baseball is a separate season. Players react differently to the pressure. There is overthinking, overanalyzing, overtrying, and overmanaging. Just throw the ball out and trust your players to perform.

Another of my dislikes is the way pitchers have been developed. It's part of the overspecialization of the game. Bill Lee and I were discussing the beginning of the specialization of pitchers back in the '70s. He quoted Buckminster Fuller, who said, "Specialization breeds extinction," and that is what's happening to starting pitchers. And it starts in the minor leagues where fewer and fewer starting pitchers are developed. Many are being trained to pitch one inning. That's sacrilege.

I cannot imagine as a young boy saying, "I want to grow up to be a big league pitcher and pitch one inning a game and maybe three innings a week." I'd rather be part of the ground crew.

I don't like deemphasizing the pitcher's job as a fielder. This is a skill which can be taught early in a pitcher's career—in high school and certainly by the time he gets to the minors. Too many pitchers don't know how to slide or run the bases properly. These are skills, which also can be taught and learned early. There is no excuse for a major leaguer who hasn't learned them. I dislike pitch counts and inning restrictions for pitchers. I wish they'd quit making rules like a relief pitcher must face a minimum of three batters. This rule handcuffs the manager from using his relievers to match up against certain batters. Please don't make a rule that does away with a very strategic part of the game. But I like Hall of Famer John Smoltz's idea that each team would be allowed no more than two mid-inning pitching changes per game.

Bring back the brushback pitch. I wasn't an intimidating pitcher, but I actually hit more batters than Bob Gibson. Gibby threw inside so he could pitch outside. Nobody does that anymore. If you throw one near a batter, you'll get ejected. There are too many mound conferences. I don't think we had frequent meetings to change the signs the catcher was flashing when runners got on base. Most pitchers today try to avoid contact.

That's understandable. It's a hitters' game, and now it's a power hitters' game, so it usually ends up a 3–2 count and a walk or strikeout or a home run. We encouraged contact because unlike today every routine fly ball didn't become a home run.

The most difficult challenge in baseball is winning over a longer period of time because you have to overcome injuries, slumps, and bad breaks. If playoffs are financially necessary for owners, end the season sooner, play fewer games, and make September a playoff month. That said, I still don't like a playoff system, which dilutes the championship. I liked it better when there were only eight teams in each league. The best teams in each league met in the World Series. Things have gotten complicated and prioritized quantity over quality with the wild-card games and divisional series. A team with the fifth or sixth best record could win the World Series. I understand that cash is king, but I don't have to like it!

Major League Baseball missed a great opportunity to take the same stance The Masters golf tournament had taken. The "Fall Classic," as we called it for years, was an American institution. People my age still talk of being able to listen to the games on a radio in school when the teacher brought one to the classroom during afternoon school hours. In my opinion the World Series could have and should have been as special as The Masters, which is the same every year and broadcast with minimal commercials. I think Major League

Baseball could have done what the leaders of the Augusta National Golf Club demanded for The Masters. Augusta laid down certain ground rules, and CBS has abided by those rules for decades. My friend, the late Larry Parker, handled the TV negotiations for The Masters for years. Peter Lund, another friend, represented CBS at the table. I arranged a lunch with them at Ekwanok Country Club in Manchester, Vermont, where Parker and I were members. Lund came as my guest. To hear Lund explain the negotiations with them, it was mostly: "Yes, Larry, we will do that. Yes, Larry, we will do that."

The Masters is a daytime activity. People set their schedules to watch it. Of course, now you can record it and watch it anytime you wish. The World Series could command the same respect if owners didn't cave to shortsighted greed. It started with Oakland A's owner Charley Finley's desire to play World Series games at night. And now with the games on past bedtime for our youth, they have lost an entire generation of fans. I am not a fan of having the World Series played at a so-called "neutral" site. This is a revenue-driven decision. That's why many older-generation fans have stopped watching or even following the game. It belongs to the hometown fans and should be played in the afternoon.

The enjoyment of today's game has diminished for older fans because of the length of time and different rules. In my opinion seven-inning games would remedy this. Fans' attention span is about two-and-a-half hours unless the game is really exciting, and not enough are. Three-and-a-half hours for one game is just too long. Seven innings could give us a chance to see complete-game pitching duels and reward a starting pitcher for his effort.

I have always enjoyed the traditions of baseball. There was a sameness to it over the years, dating back to when I first became attracted to it. I think the game has declined with the expansion from 16 teams to the current 30. The arrival of the designated hitter in the American League in 1973 (and its use in both leagues in the jerry-rigged 2020 season), batting gloves, protective equipment, tightly wound baseballs, shorter dimensions of the outfield fences, steroids, analytics, firing of scouts, highlight shows glorifying home runs, the Home Run Derby at the All-Star Game, and the drastic contraction of the minor leagues in 2020 have all detracted from the appeal and charm of the game.

I was a better-than-average hitter for a pitcher. I hit 16 home runs, was a good bunter, and I pinch ran and pinch hit on occasion. Before Greg Maddux passed me by a month, I was the oldest pitcher in the major leagues to steal a base. I was older than 41! I enjoyed being a baseball player who happened to be a pitcher. Even though I was helped by the adoption of the designated hitter because it allowed me to stay in games that were tied in the late innings and probably pick up a few more wins—and maybe a few more losses, too—I still don't like it.

There are too few hit-and-run plays, sacrifice bunts, or triples anymore. Showmanship and celebrating on the bases seem to be more important than paying attention to where the ball is. Why would you look at your teammates in the dugout while you're running down the first-base line and not pay attention to where the ball is going?

Players use new gloves which are not properly broken in. By doing so, you're not giving yourself the best chance to make a play. Many of the items on my list of dislikes are examples of how the game has become more style and less substance. In my opinion, it's a lack of respect for the uniform which the players are privileged to wear. I don't like the sloppily worn uniforms. Some of them look like track suits or pajamas. I'm disappointed that Major League Baseball has not required all players to wear their uniforms the same way. That's why they refer to them as *uniforms*, which should mean the same way in all cases. Why allow all the protective gear? This isn't football. It's embarrassing to think players have to wear all this stuff to play. And why the batting gloves? It's all my friend Hawk Harrelson's fault. He wore them because he had a blister from playing golf one day. Isn't pine tar enough to help you grip the bat?

I don't like necklaces on players. Joaquín Andújar used to wear a gold necklace to the mound at the start of the game, but the home-plate umpire would ask him to remove it because it was a distraction to the batter. Andújar knew that, but he wore it to the mound every start. It was like a touchstone, I guess. Hardly any modern players wear the sanitary white socks and the covering stirrup socks, which virtually every player wore when I played. A few wear them today and wear their pants knee-high.

I enjoy announcing a game because I am involved in every pitch. I don't think I could do a large number of games anymore as I did 20 years ago. I don't have the patience. That's my job. As a fan, I record most games and fast forward until there is a scoring situation. A lot of people say they follow the game, but they really watch highlight shows to actually see it. Truth be told: many pitchers are unhappy with all the shifting by infielders. My friend and former Major League Baseball manager Buck Showalter and many other former managers and baseball people have an idea: require two infielders on each side of second base and at least one foot on the dirt by every infielder. I like it!

Tony Kubek, a great Yankees shortstop and later a Yankee broadcaster for five seasons (1989–1993), passed his job as the analyst on the MSG Network on to me because he lost interest in the way the game was being played and operated.

I'm afraid my day of feeling that way is coming. I hope the way it is operated and played attracts a lot of new young fans. But it is far from its original concept of watching a couple of hours of action on a warm spring or summer afternoon where it was quite enough to hear the ball hit the bat sitting in the stands. I'm 83 as I write this. I am concerned about the game being appealing to young fans in years to come. I hope I'm wrong.

CHAPTER 7

The Hall of Fame

I n 1947 when I was eight years old, my parents and an aunt and uncle drove to Cooperstown, New York, to see my dad's hero, Robert Moses "Lefty" Grove, inducted into the National Baseball Hall of Fame. My second favorite piece of memorabilia is a photograph of my dad standing in front of the Hall of Fame Museum in 1947, wearing a shirt and tie with a corncob pipe in hand. (If you are wondering what my favorite piece of memorabilia is, it is the photograph of my dad and me standing on the field of Metropolitan Stadium in Bloomington, Minnesota, prior to Game 7 of the 1965 World Series. And, yes, he is wearing a suit, shirt, and tie and has his corncob pipe in his mouth.) Grove owned a bowling alley in Lonaconing, Maryland, and my family drove to Lonaconing on the way to Cooperstown. They didn't see or meet Grove.

My dad enjoyed questioning me on various baseball records, and one was always: "Who were the first five players inducted into the Hall of Fame in 1936?" I soon learned their names: Ty Cobb, Babe Ruth, Honus Wagner, Christy Mathewson, and Walter Johnson. (The five stars on the Hall's logo are said to represent these five immortals.) That was the beginning of my interest in baseball history, and I still have an interest in it. It took Grove six tries to be voted into the Hall of Fame. The voting system requires an inductee to get 75 percent of the writers' votes. At that time there were approximately 263 baseball writers voting. If you look up Grove's record, you would wonder why it took him six years to be voted in. In 17 years in the majors, he had 300 wins, 2,266 strikeouts, a 3.06 ERA, eight 20-win seasons, 35 shutouts, 298 complete games, 15 career home runs, and led the league in strikeouts in seven consecutive seasons.

But every player deemed to be Hall of Fame-worthy was judged by comparing them to the original five. Mathewson won 373 games, and Johnson won 417. That's tough competition.

Before the Covid-19 pandemic, whenever I was in a crowd of baseball fans at a memorabilia show or an awards banquet somewhere, one of the comments I got more than any other was: "You should be in the Hall of Fame." It's very flattering.

I was eligible for induction starting in 1989. Since then I have received many comments about my Hall of Fame credentials. My last season of playing was 1983. To be eligible you must have played in the major leagues for at least 10 years and be retired for five. You are then eligible to be voted on by the Baseball Writers Association of America (BBWAA) for

15 years. You need 75 percent of the votes to qualify. There are hundreds of members of the BBWAA eligible to vote. So it's really the *writers* Hall of Fame, not the *players* or owners. After following this topic and realizing how subjective selecting who belongs is, I had been amused, disappointed, annoyed, and apathetic about it.

I know many writers who are eligible to vote and respect them as baseball writers who love the game and are passionate about it. Bill Madden is a writer I have known for decades. After the results came out one year and I had dropped a few percentage points in my support, I asked him if he voted for me. I asked it more in tongue-in-cheek style because I wouldn't expect him to reveal it. He has every right to go either way despite our friendship. I followed the question up by saying that the reason I asked is that I dropped a few votes. Did I have a bad year that year? I haven't thrown a pitch in the big leagues since the middle of 1983. Why does my vote total fluctuate?

That is where my amusement in the system comes out. A majority of the writers, who are eligible to vote for Hall of Fame inductions, are incapable of deciding who should be in and who shouldn't. They should not be allowed to vote. They see the records, they follow a team, they may get thoughts from more experienced writers. I'm sure they are proud to be able to say, "I get to vote on who gets into the Baseball Hall of

Fame." But a lot of them probably never saw a game in which the eligible players played. It is the BBWAA Hall of Fame.

I have always been in awe of the players from my youth who were Hall of Famers, such as Grove, Hank Greenberg, and Ted Williams. That view has understandably changed over time as I know most of the current Hall of Famers, played against them, or have announced games the younger set of Hall of Famers played. I respect the gifts they had to be a cut above the average player. Now I'm not in awe of them but admire what they have accomplished.

My first induction in person was 1966 when Casey Stengel and Williams were inducted. An interesting side note to this was that the Hall of Fame Game that year was played between my Minnesota Twins and the St. Louis Cardinals. The Cardinals called up a 6'4" lefty to pitch against us. He was impressive. His name is Steve Carlton. He later became a good friend, a good teammate, and a Hall of Famer himself. I attended the Hall of Fame induction ceremony for my friend, Harmon Killebrew, in 1984. In 1976 I had an interesting discussion with Allen Lewis, a longtime baseball writer from Philadelphia, about Killebrew's credentials. Lewis came up to me one day and almost defiantly said, "I'm not voting for your guy Killebrew on the first ballot. All he did was hit home runs."

I didn't know if he was serious or trying to bait me into an argument. I didn't know him that well yet as it was my first season with the Philadelphia Phillies. I said, "Allen, it's too bad you never had a chance to see Harmon play in person. He hit 573 home runs, which was fifth all time when he retired after the 1975 season. And he hit them off the top pitchers in clutch situations."

The home run was a little more special during Killebrew's era, and he got in on the sixth try. Then Frank Dolson, another Philadelphia writer, began to tell me how Jim Bunning has to get in because he won more than 100 games in each league—a unique accomplishment at the time. Dolson was a delightful man, a different kind of cat who was not malicious at all. I never took the bait and started a discussion about why winning 100 in each league was more of an accomplishment than 200 in one league. Bunning, who also had a perfect game in the National League and a no-hitter in the American, and I were good friends. The night I had my teeth knocked out in 1962, he was the opposing pitcher and was the first guy to the mound after I hit the ground. He missed by one vote in 1988 at 74.2 percent. His low was 33 percent in 1982. Bunning was eventually selected by the Veterans Committee in 1996. I also attended the inductions of my teammate Mike Schmidt and Philadelphia broadcasters Harry Kalas and Richie Ashburn. I also was there for Bruce Sutter, Bert Blyleven, and my friend and broadcast partner, Bob Costas, in 2018.

I thought Marvin Miller should have been in the Hall of Fame years ago as I think Tommy John should be. The Hall of Fame is a museum of baseball history. These two have certainly been a big part of baseball history. I have heard from good sources that an executive on the Veterans Committee said, "We don't put people in the Hall of Fame just because they had surgery" in reference to John. If that is true, that person shouldn't even be associated with Major League Baseball and certainly shouldn't be allowed to vote. John won more games *after* the surgery than *before* and ended up with 288 wins. Does whoever said that have any idea the impact John has had on furthering the careers of hundreds of pitchers—as well as position players such as Paul Molitor—while achieving a Hall of Fame career himself? John risked his career to have Dr. Frank Jobe perform the now-famous Tommy John surgery in 1974.

In some ways, though, baseball is still the ultimate meritocracy. If you can play—hit, pitch, run, throw—you're in. At least in the modern times, baseball doesn't care where you're from, what color you are, or what language you speak. But baseball wants you to earn your spot on a team's roster with talent and hard work, not chemicals. When I was playing and even for some years afterward, there were some red lines, which were thought to guarantee automatic admission to the Baseball Hall of Fame. For pitchers it was 300 wins or 3,000 strikeouts. For batters it was 500 home runs or 3,000 hits.

A number of modern players achieved those marks, but for one reason or another have not been enshrined. Pete Rose has 4,256 hits but too many legal entanglements; Curt Schilling had 3,116 strikeouts but made some off-putting comments. Gary Sheffield had 509 home runs; Barry Bonds had a record 762 home runs, including 73 in 2001; Álex Rodríguez had 696 home runs and 3,115 hits; Mark McGwire had 583 home runs; Manny Ramirez had 555 home runs; David Ortiz had 541 home runs; and Rafael Palmeiro had 569 home runs, but they were all embroiled in the steroids controversy.

After 25 years as a major league pitcher, July 1, 1983, was my last game for the Cardinals. My name appeared on the National Baseball Hall of Fame writers' ballot for 15 years between 1989 and 2003. In 1993 I received a high of 29.6 percent of the votes by the Baseball Writers Association of America—well below the 75 percent needed for election. After that I was considered by various incarnations of the Hall of Fame Veterans Committee a number of times. But nothing came of it.

The Hall of Fame's Golden Days Era Committee considered a number of men who had played from 1947 to 1972: Dick Allen, Gil Hodges, Ken Boyer, Roger Maris,

Minnie Miñoso, Danny Murtaugh, Tony Oliva, Billy Pierce, and Maury Wills. I already held the record of longest span between World Series appearances—17 years between 1965 (with the Twins) and 1982 (with the Cardinals). Although this was not a record, it had been 38 years since I threw my last pitch.

I was in my home in Stuart, Florida, when I got the call from Jane Forbes Clark. The chairperson of the Hall of Fame, she is also a non-voting member of the Golden Days Era Committee. I was watching golf and football, including the long commercials, to keep my mind off the potential call. It was unexpected and overwhelming. I had given up on ever experiencing this years ago. I'm so happy that I am going in with Oliva, my friend and longtime teammate.

My election to the Hall of Fame was the honor of a lifetime. It will take me a while to respond to all the well wishes. My induction, along with Oliva, Hodges, Miñoso, Buck O'Neil, and Bud Fowler, is scheduled for July 24, 2022. Going into the National Baseball Hall of Fame is baseball's highest honor. I am humbled and grateful. It is a very special fraternity.

CHAPTER 8

Baseball Odds and Ends

A dinner party involving Bob Gibson, Tim McCarver, Sandy Koufax, and Bill White in the spring of 2002 came about because of my friendship with White. White and Gibby and their wives were motorhomers. That was their mode of travel. They convinced MaryAnn and me to do it as well. White lived near Koufax and his significant other, Jane, in the Bucks County, Pennsylvania, area in the summer.

While visiting Gibson in Jupiter, Florida, which is where Gibby went for a couple weeks in spring training to be with the St. Louis Cardinals, White mentioned that he was going up to Vero Beach, Florida, to see Koufax, who still spends his winters there. I had mentioned that to my wife, MaryAnn. White and MaryAnn were very close as they enjoyed light-hearted banter about politics. She suggested we invite them all to our home, which was halfway between Jupiter and Vero Beach, for a dinner party. All agreed. I didn't know if Gibby would be friendly because if you weren't a Cardinals player, Gibby had very little to do with you. My short tenure with the Cardinals was my connection to getting to be a friend of his. In 2002 we had a 20-year reunion of the Cardinals World Series championship team of 1982. I called McCarver, a former Cardinals catcher who lived in Sarasota, and told him of the plan. He immediately said he would drive down and bring the wine. McCarver is a wine expert.

It was a memorable evening. Koufax shared why he started playing baseball as he had actually gone to the University of Cincinnati to play basketball. The baseball team was going to make a trip south, and he thought baseball was a good way to get out of the cold weather. And I'll never forget Gibson's answer to MaryAnn's question about him hitting batters on purpose: "No, I wasn't trying to hit them; they just never moved out of the way."

McCarver and I speak frequently on the phone, and whenever that night comes up in conversation, we both agree it was one of the highlights of our lives.

• • •

I never played with or against a Black or Hispanic player in high school or college. The bigger cities in Southwest Michigan, where I lived, had Black players, but Zeeland High School never played against those schools. We played against the high school teams in much smaller towns like Coopersville, Hudsonville, Otsego, and Sparta, among others. Their teams were all White. Looking back, I wonder why I wasn't bold enough to speak up about what segregation was doing to Black people. Shame on all of us for not standing up sooner and saying that it was wrong. I stupidly just went along with it as if it was normal protocol. Shameful.

My roommate in Missoula, Montana, in the minors was Sandy Valdespino, a Black Cuban who went on to a seven-year career in the majors. He was first a teammate of mine with the Minnesota Twins (1965–67) and then he went on to play with the Houston Astros, Atlanta Braves, Seattle Pilots, Milwaukee Brewers, and Kansas City Royals.

It was a big deal when a club announced they had their first Black player on their major league roster like Pumpsie Green of the Boston Red Sox or Elston Howard of the New York Yankees. As I look back and think about the segregation I witnessed in Orlando in the late '50s and early '60s, I'm disappointed in myself for not being more proactive. On the way from our team hotel in Orlando to Tinker Field, the spring training headquarters of the Senators/Twins, we had to stop at the Sadler Hotel and pick up Lenny Green, Earl Battey, and Julio Becquer, three of our players who were Black. I roomed with a Black classmate at Hope college in Holland, Michigan, in 1957 and with Valdespino in 1958. But in Orlando in the early '60s, Blacks were not allowed to stay in the same hotel we were staying in at The Cherry Plaza.

What was I thinking? I just sat idly by and must have told myself, *That's the way it is in the South.* That was wrong thinking on my part! I should have spoken up long ago for my friends and so should all of my White teammates and the team's owners and management.

• • •

If there wasn't testing or rules against steroids, I would have been very tempted to use them. I was always a big supporter of our Players' Association, but I'm disappointed they didn't agree to testing earlier. What did they have to hide? Sports depend on integrity to get the confidence of the fans. Look at all the damage to the game that could have been avoided.

The record book has been affected by steroids use by both pitchers and hitters. Hitters don't need them today. In my opinion, it's easier to be a home run hitter today. Lighter bats, tightly-wound baseballs, the lack of brushback pitches, smaller parks, and 14-man pitching staffs with a lot of inexperienced pitchers make it easier on hitters. The top home run hitters before 2010 would have substantially higher totals. The record book is being skewed by steroids.

Ballgames now carry commercials for on-line gambling outfits. Interesting that Pete Rose was suspended because of gambling and now we promote it on baseball telecasts. Alex Rodriguez would have been banned for life under any other commissioner. If the 25th ranked player on the roster were guilty of what ARod did, would he still be allowed to be involved in the game?

• • •

I used the same glove—a Wilson A2000—for 15 seasons. It was one of the first of that model ever made. I still have it. Each spring, Wilson gave me two brand new gloves. I gave one to one of the lefties in the minors. I used the other one during pregame practice. I slathered mine with an oil called neatsfoot oil, then put two baseballs in it, and wrapped it up with thick rubber bands to get the shape and softness I liked. I never had to do anything else to it but use it.

I never started getting autographed baseballs until well into my playing career. I always felt awkward doing it. Now I wish I had because collecting has become such a big deal. I have a nice collection of autographed baseballs from many Hall of Famers with a nice personal inscription to me and from many teammates. One of my favorite signed items is an autographed fungo bat from Don Zimmer. When I asked him to do it, it brought tears to his eyes.

For the past 12 years, I have donated a lot of the funds from memorabilia signings to the Holland Community Foundation designated for the MaryAnn Kaat Memorial Fund. The proceeds from the MaryAnn Kaat Memorial Fund are used to buy equipment for youth baseball and softball in Zeeland, the home of the Jim Kaat Ballpark. I donated

$25,000 to the fund upon MaryAnn's passing and told her the day before she died that I was going to erect lights on one field in her name. The cost of the project was $75,000, and the money was raised rather quickly.

When I was playing golf with Maury Povich several years ago in Florida, one of our guys in the group mentioned what I was doing to get the lights erected. Povich mentioned what a nice gesture that was on my part. Without any thought of him responding the way he did, I said, "Thank you, we are almost there. We're $5,000 short."

After the round over a cold beer, Povich handed me a check for $5,000. He and I go back to our days with the original Washington Senators when he was an associate producer on their TV crew and his dad, Shirley, was a nationally known sports columnist and I was a 20-year-old rookie.

The Jim Kaat Ballpark, part of the 159-acre Helder Park in Zeeland, was dedicated in 2007. Helder Park has tennis courts, a dog park, basketball court, beach volleyball court, and soccer fields. The ballpark has a concession stand and bleachers for every diamond. In 2008 I appeared to hand out trophies to the winners in a Little League tournament at the ballpark named for me. I was honored to have the tournament named for me, too. I have a picture of the sign in the outfield I purchased in memory of my parents, Nancy and John. MaryAnn purchased one for me with a picture of all my grandkids. And I, of course, had the lights erected at the park in her memory.

A few years ago, I had mentioned on a podcast titled *Through The Mail* that I don't charge to sign items through the mail if they are for one's personal collection. I accept donations to the MaryAnn Kaat Memorial Fund. My agent Mike Maguire informed me that some are flouting the number of cards I sign for only $5 a card, and then some posted a picture on one of the four main websites which cater to collectors, showing a signed card of mine for a particular price that they have sold. Those were fake. I see that as exploitation that destroyed the purpose of my willingness to sign cards. As a result, I recently posted a message on all four sites that I was sorry and sad to do so, but I would be refusing mail that contained memorabilia to be signed. (I can easily tell the difference between that mail and other mail.) One collector posted a message saying he knew that wasn't me because at age 83 I wouldn't be cybersavvy enough to do that! I received a few notes thanking me for signing their cards and understanding why I stopped. They're disappointed that a few spoil things for everyone. That's the story of a lot of things in life.

One memorable souvenir I have is the ball that knocked my teeth out on July 24, 1962. It still has the teeth marks in it. I also have my original 1961 Twins jersey, too. I signed it in big letters and have it in a glass-covered shadow box all stretched out.

• • •

I want to thank the guys who I got to know even better than most of my teammates. They were referred to as "clubbies," the clubhouse attendants and more recently equipment managers.

I could probably write an entire book about the clubbies I have known. Teammates came and went. The guys who managed the clubhouse were there every year. I was in the Washington Senator/Minnesota Twins organization for 16 years. In the spring of 1961, I met a young man named Jim Wiesner. He was a batboy for the St. Paul Saints when I played in St. Paul as a member of the Charleston Senators in the Triple A American Association. With the Twins becoming a major league team in 1961, "Wies," as we all called him, was the visiting clubhouse manager. The visiting clubhouse manager came to spring training to help the home team attendant. The Twins home clubhouse man was Ray Crump, who came with the team from Washington. I was always the first one or one of the first to the park every morning in spring training. So Wies and I became friends quickly. He was without a car in Orlando and was talking about going out with some of the other clubhouse workers, but he said he had no transportation. The apartment I rented was only a short walk from Tinker Field. So I offered him my vehicle to use for the night. At about 2:00 in the morning, there was a knock on my door. It was Wies. He was trembling. I asked, "What's the matter?"

He said, "I had an accident with your car."

I said, "You look like you're all right, no injuries." He concurred. I said, "Don't worry about it. They make new cars; they don't make new yous." That kind of cemented our friendship.

Wies was very popular with visiting players because his Mom prepared the postgame spread. Today teams have their own chef, a kitchen, and a dining room in most clubhouses, but prior to those days, the postgame spread was important. After a night game, it could be difficult to find a restaurant in the city you were visiting. The highlights were the deviled eggs. I loved the way his mom made them. Wies sat in the dugout with the team until the fifth or sixth inning. When he would get up and head to the clubhouse, that was the signal that the spread had arrived.

Wies was always kind enough to send over a few deviled eggs for me. He had one of his helpers wrap them in a napkin and place them in my locker. His helpers—Jimmy Dunn and Mark McKenzie—were kids who mowed my lawn, and I helped them get on Wies' staff. Wies' spreads were by far the best in the league, according to the players. For comparative purposes, Mickey Rendine of the New York Yankees and later the New York Mets usually had pizza for us after the game. If the game ran a little long, Rendine would put the pizzas in the clothes dryer—box and all—so they'd be warm after the game. Wies passed away in 2017 at age 77. Of all the clubhouse guys I met and became friends with, Wies was the one with whom I had the longest and closet relationship.

I also was tight with Buddy Bates and Frank Coppenbarger in St. Louis near the end of my career. In 1983 it was apparent my Cardinals days were coming to an end. When I walked in the clubhouse, they would look at me and say, "Are you still here? I thought we released you yesterday."

I would look at my locker and see the uniform jersey hanging there. I said, "No. I made it for another day. I'll make it to July 4." We had a small pool of a few dollars to see who was the closest to the day the Cardinals released me. It was July 6. I won the pool. You would have to know dark clubhouse humor to understand how we could joke about someone being fired, but that's the way we rolled. Coppenbarger is a good friend I see periodically, and Bates lives in the same city as I do in Florida.

As part of that humor, we'd do a lot of locker room pranks. If a single player came to the park with dressier clothes than he was accustomed to wearing, we knew he had a date after the game. When the game started, one of us would go to his locker, take his shoes, fill them up with about an inch of water, and put them in the freezer. Then with two outs in the ninth inning, we would have the clubhouse man take them out of the freezer and put them in his locker. That usually got some loud words from the victim. We would always offer to buy him a new pair of shoes.

• • •

The Minnesota Twins had a very important game in 1967. Marty Springstead was the home-plate umpire. Our bench was not happy with some calls and began to chirp a little too loudly. Springstead walked toward our dugout, pointed at me, and said: "Get out. You're gone!" *Why me? I hadn't say a word.* I knew better than to get caught chirping at an umpire. I'd pay for that the next time I pitched, and he was behind the plate. The next time I saw Springstead, I asked him why he tossed me. He had a good explanation. He said, "I knew it was an important game for your team and I didn't want to toss a player who was in the game or might be used. I knew you had pitched the day before so I tossed you because I knew you wouldn't be used, and that would quiet things down."

I shot back, tongue in cheek, "You should have tossed Dino [Dean Chance]. I could pinch hit or pinch run. Dino couldn't do either one."

Springstead and I became good friends after his umpiring days as he became a supervisor of umpires, and I'd see him at the ballpark from time to time. Ed Runge was an American League umpire from 1954 to 1970. His son, Paul, was a National League umpire from 1973 to 1997. When Paul was behind the plate, the zone was a lot like his dad's. Batters knew they had to swing the bat. We could sure use that today. It made for a crisper game, and there seemed to be more action in the game. Batters weren't taking as many pitches. Ed's grandson, Brian, also umpired in the big leagues from 1999 to 2012. I was announcing games then and went to the umpires' room one day when Brian was part of the umpiring crew. He said, "I can't call strikes like my grandpa and dad did." The umpires were graded on their performance every game. If their percentage of mistakes reached a certain level consistently, their job was in jeopardy. Too bad. I liked the human element better. It got batters in the frame of mind to swing the bat instead of all the 3-2 counts and bases on balls you see today.

When I played, players became quite friendly with the umpires. There were not as many teams, and each league had their own umpires. There was no electronic big brother looking over their shoulders then. So each umpires had his own interpretation of the strike zone. Ed was the pitcher's favorite home-plate umpire. He had a generous strike zone, and his opening remark when the first batter of the game stepped into the batter's box was: "The fans didn't come here to see you walk. Swing the bat."

An indication of how his strike zone influenced the game was the 1967 All-Star Game. It went 15 innings, and the National League won 2–1. There were two bases-on-balls issued, 30 strikeouts, and the extra-inning game was played in three hours and 41 minutes. They swung the bat, but they were facing elite pitchers (Juan Marichal, Bob Gibson, Don Drysdale, Tom Seaver, Mike Cuellar, and Catfish Hunter, to name just a few). Elite pitchers will usually dominate all hitters.

On the other side of the coin was Eddie Hurley. He had a strike zone the size of a cereal box. There were no corners on Hurley's plate. He was a nice guy, friendly with everyone. When he was the first-base umpire in Minnesota, I would often find a place on the far end and top step of our first-base dugout to watch the game the night or day before I was scheduled to pitch. With Hurley umpiring first, it meant he would be the umpire behind the plate in my start. He always had a pocketful of hard candy. Between innings he would saunter over to our dugout and give me a few candies. I'd collect them and put them in my jacket pocket. About the eighth inning, I'd have at least a dozen of them. When he came over to the dugout, I showed him all the candies he'd given me. "Eddie," I said, "Can I trade these candies in for a dozen borderline strikes tomorrow?"

He'd get a good chuckle out of that, but he never increased the size of his strike zone.

He was the home-plate umpire in Game Seven of the 1965 World Series when I started against the Los Angeles Dodgers and Sandy Koufax. I told Earl Battey, our catcher, to just set up behind the middle of the plate. There was no need to look for corners with Hurley behind the plate.

• • •

I preferred pitching in day games because it's tougher for a batter to pick up the ball than in a night game. As cable television became a bigger part of baseball broadcasting and more teams owned their own cable outlets outright, more and more games became night games. Between innings, I didn't have a preference for where I sat. Sometimes I chatted with my catcher, but mostly I stayed in my own world. If I was on a winning streak at home, I always drove the same route from my house to the ballpark.

I never had a set seat when we traveled by plane. With the Philadelphia Phillies, we had several bridge players, including Tim McCarver, the most accomplished player, along with Bruce Keidan, a sportswriter. How about that? We were actually friends with sportswriters and mingled with them in those days! Garry Maddox, Mike Schmidt, Jim Lonborg, and

Davey Johnson also played bridge. We would rotate in and out so everyone got to play. We folded some of our seatbacks down and made our own card table. I used to sit next to Jim Holt a lot when I was with the Minnesota Twins. We played gin rummy.

CHAPTER 9
Travel

Fred Cox, a kicker for the Minnesota Vikings, invited to me to play golf one afternoon in 1970 after an award luncheon in Minneapolis. I had never played much. That's when I started, and I got hooked on it quickly. I just learned by continually playing. My golf partners with the Minnesota Twins were Ron Perranoski, Tom Tischinski, roommate Danny Thompson, and occasionally Brant Alyea. I played with Hawk Harrelson a few times during our careers and later in Florida.

I learned to play golf right-handed because lefty clubs were not mass produced. Experts always considered golf to be a right-hander's game. Instructors back then felt the lead arm should be the dominant arm. In my case that's my left arm. The stretching motion of the right-handed golf swing seemed to be good for my arm. I didn't play 18 holes every day during my playing career, but I tried to make some swings and hit some balls every day. My favorite courses were Pebble Beach in California; Firestone in Akron, Ohio; Mission Hills on the Kansas side of Kansas City; and Woodhill in Minneapolis.

In December of 2013 at age 75 at the McArthur Golf Club in Hobe Sound, Florida, I shot 75 both as a lefty and righty in the same week. Golf historians say that I am the only person to have done that.

Right after the terrorist attacks on September 11, 2001, we rented a small RV, bought a starter unit, and moved up to a 38-foot diesel a few years later. We looked at where family and friends lived and also where we knew golf friends who would set up golf at the clubs they belonged. I travel with two sets of XXIO clubs—lightweight clubs designed for seniors like me with slower swing speeds. One set is lefty, and one righty. I use both. We had taken RV trips to Maine after the baseball season. Those gave us an idea of whether we liked it and could handle the driving and finding places to stop and refuel, etc. We found it to be a great way to travel.

We had navigation and some helpful maps and guidebooks for RVs. In the fall of 2007, my wife, MaryAnn, and I travelled around the country in a 38-foot Itasca motor home. We traversed 10,000 miles covering 27 states. I played more than 60 different golf courses from Maine to Oregon, Southern California to Texas, and then back to Florida. MaryAnn wasn't a golfer. She read and brushed our three cats: Samantha, Hot Shot, and Lover Boy. It was fun to observe the way they looked out the windows and found their little favorite resting spots. (Yes, Kitty Kaat has three kitty cats.)

MaryAnn and I split the driving. Our RV was not really that difficult to drive. You just keep your distance behind other vehicles on the road because it takes a while to stop. I also would recommend practicing pulling out into traffic, passing, making turns because you need a lot of room, and trying to park somewhere where you don't have to back up.

The year 2007 was the final one of MaryAnn's life as she was battling bladder cancer. That's the reason I left broadcasting. I still hadn't retired. I did some blogging for YES Network in 2007 and 2008. I offered to return to YES after MaryAnn passed away in July of 2008, but John Filippelli, the executive producer, was not interested. He and I developed an adversarial relationship because he was always trying to put words in my mouth to please George Steinbrenner. I refused to compromise my credibility, as I was taught by Bill White. I was not a homer. I wasn't retiring, just stepping away to tend to MaryAnn. She had negotiated a deal for me with YES for me to do enough work, blogging, and making appearances with sponsors on behalf of YES to earn enough money to maintain my health insurance. MaryAnn passed away in July of 2008. My YES days were over. With covering the Yankees in my rearview mirror, and the new opportunity with the MLB network at age 70, I had started a new chapter in my life. Using Clint Eastwood's attitude as my model, I had no plans to retire but had to find ways to use the skills I was gifted with, which was commenting on baseball games.

In the early 2000s while having breakfast at the Osceola Café in Stuart, Florida, with my friend, Jack MacAleese, I had been introduced to Margie Bowes, a golf professional who worked at nearby Willoughby Golf Club in Stuart. Jack and his wife Marge were members of Willoughby. Margie was passing our table, and Jack stopped her and introduced us. As Margie told me later when she saw Jack at the club a few days later, she asked, "What's his status?"

Jack's answer was: "He's very married." Margie said, "I thought so."

Time passed, and Margie heard that MaryAnn had passed away the prior year in 2008. She saw me at a golf event and offered condolences. Some months later she asked Jack: "Is Jim seeing anyone?"

I was not. My plan was to drive around the country and play golf in my newly purchased RoadTrek, which was a high-end sprinter van, perfect for one person to use as a home while traveling. He asked if I'd like to join him and Marge for dinner and meet Margie Bowes. I agreed. We met at Willoughby a short time later. This was in the spring of 2009. Marge MacAleese was telling me how Margie had helped her with her short game. I asked Margie if she had time to give me a lesson. She did, and I saw her a few days later at

Willoughby for the lesson. After we finished I asked, "What do I owe you?"

She said, "Oh, nothing. Just take me out to dinner." The wily ways of a woman! I will fast forward to give you an idea of how things moved along in our relationship. We were married 70 days after that dinner at Willoughby.

Margie was widowed at age 37, had no children, and never remarried after her husband Billy passed away from a rare cancer at age 39. I had called my brother-in-law, John Montanaro, the brother of my late wife. He always called me the brother he never had. I said, "John, I am seeing a lady, and it's getting serious. I don't want to do anything inappropriate out of respect for MaryAnn." His answer was the best news one could wish for. He told me that I had made his sister the happiest he had ever seen her, and I deserved to move forward and be happy.

Margie's summer position was heading the ladies' golf program at Salem Country Club in Peabody, Massachusetts. So in late May, she headed to Massachusetts for the start of the golf season at Salem. I joined her a few weeks later while motoring up in my RoadTrek. We discussed marriage after I met her dad and brothers and was "approved." We thought about waiting until the fall and getting married in Florida. Margie didn't like the idea of having to travel on weekends to meet me wherever my schedule took me, so I said, "Do you want to get married next week?"

I was committed to pitch in the Hall of Fame Game in Cooperstown, New York, with Bob Feller and Bill Lee on the 20th of June. She had to make sure her boss, Kevin Wood, the head professional at Salem, could find a replacement for her. He did, and we got married in a small ceremony in Bennington, Vermont, Margie's hometown. Then we went off to Cooperstown for our honeymoon and a new life together.

Bob Feller was 90 when he pitched in the Hall of Fame game in 2009. He trained all winter to be able to throw the ball from 60'6" and he did quite well. Hall of Famer Paul Molitor was on our team and went up to bat against Feller. We pleaded with Molly: "Please don't hit a ball up the middle." Everyone was respectful of *not* hitting one back at "Rapid Robert," as he was called in his pitching days. As the first major leaguer to enlist, he missed four years in the prime of his career when he joined the U.S. Navy in 1941. Feller was awarded eight battle stars for his service on the battleship *USS Alabama* during the war. Margie invited her dad, Chuck Mather, and a couple of her brothers to come to Cooperstown for the weekend. Mather served on the *USS Missouri* at the same time Feller was on the *USS Alabama*. Feller signed a ball to Mather that said, "from one battleship sailor to another."

Mather passed away in 2011, but Margie still has that ball on her desk.

The year 2009 was quite a year for me. From getting back in the booth and announcing the World Baseball Classic in Puerto Rico, to beginning to do MLB games with Bob Costas, to getting married to Margie Mather Bowes, to being nominated for an Emmy, it was a whirlwind.

I had made commitments to appear at several functions prior to meeting Margie. One was to be a guest pitching coach for the Hannibal, Missouri, entry in the summer collegiate league. It was a favor to my friend Roland Hemond, the general manager of the Chicago White Sox when I played with them in the mid-1970s.

His son, Jay Hemond, was the manager of the team, the Hannibal Cavemen. It was for college players who wanted to boost their draft status to the scouts in attendance at those games. Margie and I toured the Midwest in my RoadTrek but stayed in hotels or motels along the way. We called it our $100,000 clothes closet. I appeared at the Bob Feller Museum in Feller's hometown of Van Meter, Iowa. That's where I met Mike Maguire, who booked my signing appearances and does to this day. A conscientious, caring man, he has been so helpful to me.

I announced the Futures Game in St. Louis for the MLB Network prior to the 2009 All-Star Game. I had a speaking engagement in Sioux Falls at a sports dinner and then got some golf in at Whistling Straits in Wisconsin. I then went on to Chicago to do a Cubs game for the MLB Network. I went through Michigan to see my family and on to Newburyport, Massachusetts, where Margie lived in the summer while working at Salem Country Club. I did a Boston Red Sox game at Fenway Park and met Terry "Tito" Francona on the field. Tito and I have been buddies for years. I knew his father well and pitched against both of them during my career. Tito signed a uniform shirt for Margie that she still has hanging in her closet. Yes, she was a Red Sox fan. We spent the last weeks of the summer in Newburyport, and I traveled from there to do the remainder of my MLB games. Costas and I were getting to know each other better each game and developed a nice chemistry. It's even stronger today. It has been quite an honor to partner with one of the best known and talented broadcasters in the country.

My late wife, MaryAnn, was not interested in international travel. Of Italian descent, MaryAnn did take me on trip to Italy after the 1992 World Series, and we crossed paths with World Series hero Joe Carter. But mostly she loved being at home and tending to her hibiscus and impatiens and other flowers. Margie, however, was very interested in traveling, and I was as well. Our thinking was with me being 71 and healthy that we needed to do it then. Margie is 17 years my junior but light years my senior in intelligence. So we began to plan some trips. There was group travel for us. We planned it ourselves and did it as a couple. Being of Dutch descent, I always wanted to go to the Netherlands and see the birthplace of my paternal grandparents. I never met them as they had passed away before I was born. They came to the United States—as many immigrants did—by ship when they were teenagers and settled in Grand Rapids, Michigan. That was the beginning of the Kaat family.

Paris was a city we needed to see as well. So our first trip in 2010 was to Paris and Amsterdam. While in Amsterdam I hired a car and went to Tholen, a small city in the province of Zeeland, where my grandfather was born. My grandmother was from Belgium just across the border. Since I grew up in a community where many of the Dutch settled, the names of towns in Michigan are named for them. I was born and raised in Zeeland, Michigan. The only regret I have is while in France we did not go to Normandy. That is still a desire.

I've had the great fortune to go to many great international destinations, starting during my playing days. In the winter of 1969, I visited the Philippines for a missionary organization called Overseas Crusades. I also managed to look in on Filipino baseball. The coaching experience wasn't an impactful one for the Filipino team. It participated in the Asian games against China, Japan, and Taiwan. I spent a few days with the players mostly talking about baseball history and finding out what they knew about it. Babe Ruth had played in Rizal Stadium when he was there on a servicemen's tour with a lot of celebrities during World War II.

In 2011 Margie and I decided to visit Australia and New Zealand. Well, if you're going that far, you need to spend a lot of time there. Australia is a big country! We spent three weeks in each. We spent a few days on Orpheus Island on the Great Barrier Reef and went snorkeling and fishing. She has started to transition from a skilled professional golfer to a fly fisherwoman. In fact, by 2021, she was strictly interested in fishing and has given up golf for the most part.

Our trip to Australia and New Zealand in 2012 was a combination of golfing, fishing, and seeing the Great Barrier Reef. I spent a little time finding out what the interest level of baseball was in those countries. We liked Brisbane, Australia. I had two birthdays because we left on November 7 and arrived in Brisbane on November 7. Melbourne was nice and more Americanized than we expected. Sydney is a wonderful city. I even attended a performance of *Swan Lake*.

Australia has had a professional baseball league since 1989 and produced several major league players. Dave Nillson, a catcher for the Milwaukee Brewers, is thought to be the first. I met a few Americans involved in baseball while we were there. Through longtime pro golfer and current golf analyst,

Ian Baker Finch, whom I met and golfed with in Florida, I was able to contact some golf clubs in Australia. We played Kingston Heath, Royal Melbourne, and Metropolitan, which are well-known courses in the Melbourne area. I also looked into what was going on with their baseball program. I made contact with the office of the Melbourne Aces and found out that Jonathan Schuerholz, son of Hall of Fame executive John Schuerholz, was the manager, and Mike Krukow's daughter, Tessa, worked in the front office. Mike was a big league pitcher for 14 years and is a friend. I watched the home run hitting contest that some of the Aussie rugby teams staged before one game and broadcast their All-Star Game on Australian national radio, their version of ESPN Radio.

After a stay in Sydney for a few days, we left for Auckland, New Zealand. A tragic event occurred when we were in Sydney. I walked out of my hotel room on the morning of December 14, 2012, and a man leaving his room told me about the Sandy Hook shooting that took place that day. I was not very proud to be an American that day.

I went on to New Zealand for a little golf at Julian Robertson's famous golf resorts called Cape Kidnappers and Kauri Cliffs. Robertson is a billionaire hedge fund manager who developed these resorts on the North Island. He owns the Matakauri Lodge, which, alas, has no golf course, on the South Island near Queenstown.

After 10 days on the North Island, we landed in Auckland, which most travelers do. It's the largest city in New Zealand. As the saying goes, New Zealand has four million people and 40 million sheep. Sixty percent of the people live in Auckland on the North Island. Then we went on to the South Island. We liked Australia and liked the North Island of New Zealand even a little more than Australia, but we loved the South Island. I had looked forward to seeing New Zealand for a long time. It's so far away and not talked about a lot in the USA. It has wonderful people and beautiful countryside. The people are so friendly and humble that it reminded me of what the USA was like when I grew up in a small Midwestern town in the '40s and '50s.

Auckland is New Zealand's major city and is growing beyond its infrastructure. It has a lot of traffic issues now. A few things we could learn from the Kiwis: Air New Zealand knows how to load an airplane. There's none of this clogging up an aisle and stuffing multiple carry-ons into the overhead bins to make the loading process as long as the flight, as passengers are allowed to do on flights in the USA. We are the greatest country in the world. We put a man on the moon, but we can't be efficient at loading an airplane. And the crosswalks are better, too. Have you ever driven in a major city and had to turn right at an intersection, but the walk sign was on, and by the time all the pedestrians had crossed the street, the traffic light was red again? Well, what amazed me was something I saw for the first time in Auckland. All traffic lights say walk for a minute or two, and you can walk in all four directions and also walk diagonally from corner to corner. Then all signs say stop, and traffic flows free—first north to south and then east to west. It's simple and efficient. What a concept! It just requires a little patience.

We spent just a day in Auckland as Margie was eager to head to the Tongariro River to fly fish. We had rented an SUV to tour from place to place and then took a flight to Queenstown and a helicopter trip through the Milford Sound. They filmed *The Lord of the Rings* there. Jay Robertson, Julian's son, arranged the trip with a helicopter company that he used. It had the most spectacular, desolate mountains and land I've ever witnessed. You would never think there was that much undeveloped territory in the world. While in Queenstown we played golf at Jack's Point, a course that was public at the time. Margie and I still bring it up when mentioning some of the best courses we have played.

I was gradually learning the names of people in charge of Baseball International. Robert Eenhoorn was the CEO of Dutch baseball. A Dutch native, Eenhoorn was Derek Jeter's backup briefly in the mid-1990s. The Netherlands has the most productive baseball program in Europe. They have won many European championships and they have great programs for kids. He showed me the facility they have in Haarlem. They use a smaller ball for the youngest kids and gradually increase the size for the older ones. Where are we with that thinking in our country? I have suggested it to Steve Keener, president of the U.S. Little League. One of the biggest issues with youth baseball in the USA is that the ball is too big for a lot of kids, and the diamonds are too big. We should downsize everything.

I am very impressed with girls' fast-pitch softball. My granddaughter, Casey, played on a New Jersey championship softball team. My son-in-law, Peter, invited me to speak to Casey's team and watch them play. I was anticipating a slow mistake-filled game with limited skills by the girls. I was pleasantly surprised about how well-coached they were in the fundamentals. It was a well-played, fast-paced game, so kids and parents don't get bored. Give me a young girls' softball game to watch any day over a boys' Little League game with its high percentage of walks and errors.

I had seen teams from other countries—like the Dominican Republic, Venezuela, and Puerto Rico—where baseball was actually more popular than it is in the USA. The sport is gaining in popularity in Italy, China, and even Israel. I finally located the name of the person in charge of the New Zealand program: Ryan Flynn. A former minor league player who enjoyed traveling around the world, Flynn accepted the position as CEO of New Zealand baseball in 2012. Flynn had been the head of the Guam baseball program for a few years prior to that. I contacted Flynn about the possibility of coming to New Zealand for a while and staging some clinics for their young pitchers. He liked the idea.

The problem was the financing. MLB International was hesitant to invest too much money into New Zealand baseball because it didn't know what the sustainability would be in that country. Fast-pitch softball was more popular, but there was no future in professional softball. Many of the kids, though, were beginning to dream about being big league baseball players. I appealed to Chris Park and Jim Small and even Kim Ng, the general manager for the Miami Marlins. Ng was a friend from our days together in Yankeeland. But I got the same response about it being hard to justify investing so much money in a program with an uncertain future. For example, Taiwan has 200,000 kids playing youth baseball. New Zealand had fewer than 1,000 when Flynn took over the program. Mark Melancon, Chris Woodward, Didi Gregorius, and a few others had traveled there on their own. Woodward was the manager of New Zealand's national team for a while and received some compensation, but if one wished to go there, it would be on his or her own nickel. I appealed to Dan Foster, CEO of the Major League Players Alumni Association, of which I was the president years ago. Foster said the alumni association made some funds available in exchange for wearing the alumni logo gear and giving clinics as an alumni rep. With that and our own money, Margie and I decided to plan a two-and-a-half-month trip to New Zealand.

We spent a few days in Auckland with Flynn and some of his staff. We also met Doug White, who has become a friend. White is the head golf professional at Titarangi Golf Club, the only Alistair Mackenzie-designed course in New Zealand. He is a huge baseball fan. And he's huge in more ways than one. White is 6'8" and built like a tight end. He had aspirations of playing for the All Blacks, the world famous championship rugby team in New Zealand. He has visited us in Vermont for baseball games and golf.

I staged a pitching clinic for the New Zealand National Team players and a lot of their coaches and met several of the coaches. It was interesting to watch their pitchers go through their motions. A lot of the coaches are influenced by Japanese baseball. Japanese pitchers tend to drop their pitching arm straight down the outside of the back leg and curl the palm upward. They believe that that technique helps them hide the ball from the batter. I don't buy that theory. In the USA we would call these types of pitchers "hookers." My friend Rick Sutcliffe was a "hooker." Sutcliffe is 6'7", and with his big frame, he pitched that way for 18 years and won 171 games. So it can be an effective way to pitch. The danger is that by dropping the arm down you need to curl the palm inward and bring it back up over your head and back. That means your elbow makes a lot of stops and starts. I did it myself for a few years early in my career. I wish I had learned the out and up of the glove arm action when I was younger. It would have had less elbow stress, been more efficient, and produced more arm speed. No pitcher or coach has ever asked me about that motion except Leo Mazzone, the former Atlanta Braves and Baltimore Orioles pitching coach. Mazzone is a disciple of Johnny Sain like me and understood the pitching motion.

It would be futile to try to sell that to today's coaches and pitchers because they believe speed and power come from other sources. Arm speed has always been more important to me than power. You need muscle strength to create speed, but you can get that with simple internal and external rotations on a circuit training device with as little as a five-pound weight. You develop it in your lower body by going through your pitching motion day after day off a mound and a pitching rubber as you do in a game.

I'm fortunate to have pitched in the major leagues for 25 seasons because it took me a while to figure out what worked and what didn't. I learned a lot as I went along and thankfully crossed paths with Eddie Lopat in 1961 and Sain in 1965. Sain was my pitching coach in 1965 and 1966 and again in 1973, '74, and '75. If you check my record during those years, you would think I was Sandy Koufax. I wish I could have had him as my pitching coach for all 25 seasons. Others meant well and always tried to help other pitchers and me. No coach purposely tries to hurt a pitcher's effectiveness. But Lopat and Sain made the most impact on my career.

Anyhow, we went to the South Island for a few weeks in Nelson, New Zealand. We had researched Nelson before leaving for New Zealand. Right on the shore of Tasman Bay, it has a population of a little more 50,000 and is the oldest city on the South Island. It's often called "Sunny" Nelson because of the amount of sunshine there. The population is very athletic. People wind surf, paraglide, run along the shore, and sail. It has the potential to have a Pebble Beach type of course because it's right along the shore of the bay with lots of wind.

We had booked an Airbnb owned by Dennis Doljes, who was born and raised outside of Cleveland, Ohio. He met us at the airport and made sure we got the right rental vehicle. He knew all the locals. His father emigrated from the U.S. in 1965 when he was a young boy. He owned a nice apartment overlooking Tasman Bay, and it was perfect for our needs. The story of his parents emigrating to New Zealand is worth telling. Ed Doljes passed in 2019 last year at age 90.

Ed had been successful in the construction business in Ohio. He and his wife, Ruthie, decided they wanted to find a place somewhere in the world that had a nice year-round climate where they could live permanently. They read several books on New Zealand and on Nelson. The more they read about Nelson, the clearer it became that Nelson was the place to live.

In 1965 Ed and Ruthie boarded a ship with their kids and sailed from Los Angeles to Auckland. Ed found out softball was a big sport in New Zealand. He was an excellent softball player in Ohio. When Ed passed away on November 5, 2019, he had been awarded every honor a softball coach could have. The New Zealand women's softball team won many national championships under his guidance. Dennis arranged for me to have lunch with Ed during our stay in Nelson. We exchanged a lot of baseball stories over lunch.

I think we live in the greatest country in the world despite our flaws and I had a great childhood in Zeeland, Michigan, and had great parents. But knowing what I know now after visiting Nelson, I would not have been disappointed to grow up there. It's a special place. One of the Nelson youth baseball coaches is Marty Grant, who was ranked as the top fast-pitch softball pitcher in the world at one time. American companies would hire Grant to come to the U.S. and pitch for their teams. They give him a job for a few hours a week so he could pitch for them. As a young boy, fast-pitch softball was my first organized sport. Every little town in southwest Michigan had a softball team. Marty's son, Cooper, is the most talented young player for his age in Nelson and maybe in all of New Zealand. I hope Coop gets a college scholarship to play baseball in the U.S.

Baseball is so new in New Zealand and needs so much help: Nelson doesn't have a diamond with bases and a backstop or a pitcher's mound. That's why I appealed to MLB International to help them. Under Flynn's leadership, New Zealand now has a team in the Australian Baseball League called the Auckland Tuataras. What's a Tuatara? It's a lizard-like reptile that is endemic to New Zealand.

I had a wonderful three weeks in Nelson, where I met many wonderful people. Several were expatriates who wanted to leave the USA after 9/11 and had done well enough in their careers to move to New Zealand. Tom Kroos from Sheboygan, Wisconsin, became a great friend. He's the president of Nelson Baseball. He is a biologist who makes sure the New Zealand waters are nice and clean and good for fishing. He and Margie became fast friends. A dedicated woman and good softball player, Rachel Knowles is one of the coaches. I kept a close eye on a young pitcher named James Matthews. He was just nine and had a perfect pitching motion. I asked Kroos who that youngster was, and Matthews' mother overheard me. She thought James had done something wrong. She quickly came to see me. Despite him having the best pitching motion there, I found out he just started playing.

He was a cricket bowler, which is the same as a baseball pitcher, but he felt cricket was too slow so he wanted to play baseball.

New Zealand baseball fans can see baseball games on ESPN or FOX Sports or stream them by buying a subscription from MLBTV, a huge source of revenue for MLB club owners. I always thought if I could spend some time with one of the New Zealand professional cricket bowlers and teach them the pitching motion, they might become good big league pitchers. Dustin Hamilton was a young lefty who helped coach the Nelson kids. He also helped coach the pitchers.

I met Freddie Flintoff in the early 2000s at a golf club in Florida. After playing golf we had an adult beverage or two and compared the motion of a cricket bowler and a baseball pitcher. Flintoff was one of the best or quite possibly the best cricket bowler in the United Kingdom. He's 6'3", 215 pounds and solid as a rock. A lot of the cricket bowlers tear up their shoulders because they put so much stress on the shoulder joint. I could see Flintoff being like Gerrit Cole. Flintoff is in his mid-40s now and is a TV/radio commentator.

After planning our entire 2017 trip from Stuart, Florida, to San Francisco to Auckland, New Zealand, we were ready to go on December 31. The planning included bed and breakfasts or vacation rentals, car rentals, transportation within New Zealand, and people to meet for baseball, fishing, and golf. Since it is a 14½-hour flight, we decided to fly to San Francisco a couple days in advance. It's a good thing we did. A mechanical issue delayed our departure out of Palm Beach to Atlanta, and we missed our connection in Atlanta. So we arrived in San Francisco on January 1 and left for Auckland on January 2. We love Air New Zealand. It's an efficient and polite service within New Zealand as well. The first surprise when we arrived in New Zealand was at customs. Margie's fishing boots and waders took extra examination. New Zealand is very meticulous about the condition of their waters, and they disinfect those items at customs.

After a great trip, we flew from Auckland to San Francisco on March 9 and began our orientation back to U.S. time. I was scheduled to announce the World Baseball Classic pool in San Diego from March 14–19 and then the semifinals and finals at Dodger Stadium in Los Angeles on March 21 and 22. That has become an enjoyable event for me as you see the international teams and players who have become such a big part of baseball. I saw Kenley Jansen, the star reliever for the Los Angeles Dodgers, when he was a catcher for the Dutch National Team in 2009. His team defeated the Dominican Republic. The United States team defeated Puerto Rico to win the WBC in 2017, but international teams are getting stronger every year. The Covid-19 pandemic caused the 2021

WBC to be canceled. I have announced games the past three classics in 2009, 2013, and 2017 and would love to do it again.

In addition to Australia and New Zealand, we also explored the United Kingdom. In 2013 we took a golf/touring trip to Ireland. I was a member of the Fox Golf Club in Palm City, Florida, near my home in Stuart. Our managing partner was Eoghan O'Connell. A Walker Cup player for the European team and a collegiate golfer at Wake Forest, he and I became good friends. He grew up in Ireland. O'Connell arranged our golf trip for us with recommendations for golf and sightseeing. A Guinness at Dick Mack's Pub in Dingle is a must. An American woman was celebrating her birthday while we were there, and it was quite a songfest.

The southern swing of Irish golf courses is the most popular with Americans because of accessibility. A flight to Shannon, Ireland, from New York is the same amount of time as a flight from New York to L.A. Adare Manor, American-owned and site of a future Ryder Cup, is a good starting point. We hired a driver and spent two weeks playing the usual courses that visitors play. We played Lahinch, Tralee, and later Ballybunion. We played the latter twice—once in a sideways rain and once on a clear day. O'Connell's dad, Tim Joe, hosted us there. Killarney and Old Head have the most spectacular scenery you could imagine, and then Waterville and Dooks are lesser known but enjoyable courses. A golf trip to Ireland has always been on the wish list of most golfers, and we're glad we went and enjoyed the golf, the people, the countryside, and Dick Mack's Pub.

In May of 2014, we took a golf trip to Scotland. My friend and well known Canadian golf writer Lorne Rubenstein wrote a book titled *A Season in Dornoch: Golf and Life in the Scottish Highlands*. He and his wife, Nell, lived above the bookstore in Dornoch for the summer, and Lorne wrote about that special area. It's golf's birthplace and the home of famed architect Donald Ross, who helped design Royal Dornoch, which is one of my favorite courses. The Old Course, St. Andrews, is the most historic course in the world, but many locals list Royal Dornoch as a more enjoyable course. Tom Watson said it was the most fun he's had on a course. I don't know if I would call it fun, but the setting and the challenge are what I enjoyed. The Links House was a church manse that Chicago businessman Todd Warnoch turned into a boutique hotel. At the time in 2014, we were the guests that stayed there the longest period of time—10 days. We flew into Edinburgh and spent a couple days there, which I would recommend to everyone who travels to Scotland. We spent a couple nights at the Balmoral hotel, where J. K. Rowling did some of her writing for her books about Harry Potter in one of their suites. That hotel is a special treat. Edinburgh Castle is a must. On the walk up from Balmoral, I suddenly heard, "Hey, Kitty."

There are few—if any—Scots who know my nickname, so it had to be a baseball fan from America. It was a White Sox fan who recognized me and stopped to pose for a picture.

Courses like Castle Stewart, Nairn, Tain, Golspie, and Brora are lesser-known courses on the world stage but unique and enjoyable. Brora, a 20-minute drive from Dornoch, is unique in that cows have grazing rights on the course, and you may have to wait for one or two of them to trundle past the tee box before you play. The Carnegie Club at Skibo Castle is a famous destination. Many Americans have non-resident memberships. It was the home of Andrew Carnegie. Madonna married Guy Ritchie there in 2000. The highlight of the trip for me was playing Royal Dornoch multiple times. For Margie it was the chance to fish the waters in the Highlands. I'd still like to go to St. Andrews, but I'm very happy we experienced Dornoch.

CHAPTER 10

The 2021 Season

I was glad to put the Covid-abbreviated 2020 season in the rearview mirror. A season of only 60 games can hardly be considered a season. Also, all the changes made to the game nearly made it unrecognizable: doubleheader games of only seven innings, no fans in the stands, every team's regular broadcasters broadcasting from their home stadiums, the so-called "ghost" runner on second base to start the 10th inning. I am glad that the experimental ghost runner introduced in extra-inning games in 2020 was not used in the 2021 postseason.

Thinking back, sometimes I wish Major League Baseball didn't have a season in 2020. Sixty games? That's like playing 40 holes at The Masters and celebrating like you actually won it. Not legitimate. It should have been started earlier so they could have played at least 100 games. Stubborn leadership on both sides prevented that from happening. Actually, in today's sports world, 100 to 125 seven-inning games would be enough. When baseball played 154 with eight teams in each league, it was the only game in town, so to speak. Now all the seasons overlap, and 162 games is too many.

The 2021 season came down to a one-game playoff on October 5 between the New York Yankees and Boston Red Sox at Fenway Park. What could be better? Boston won 6–2. The Los Angeles Dodgers–St. Louis Cardinals wild-card game on October 6 came down to the bottom of the ninth inning with the game tied at one and two outs. Chris Taylor ended it with a walk-off two-run home run. Does baseball get more dramatic than that?

However, there were some disappointing parts of the 2021 season. With the friendly atmosphere on the field between players, some games look like they're intrasquad practice games. Players on opposite teams constantly talk to one another. Other teams appear to have no interest in being contending teams and traded away their star players.

A lack of contact and no desire to beat the shift made for long periods of time where a ball was not put in play. Constant trips to the mound by catchers and pitching coaches added to the boredom of many games. The 2021 season also had many long winning and losing streaks and tons of no-hitters—*nine!*

The influence of science is evident. With overthinking and input from the dugout and the analytics department, games lack a rhythm. That might be why no managers were fired in 2021. Managers are taking orders from upstairs. If teams made a change, they'd have to fire a lot of people. Perhaps as a result of these issues, attendance and viewer and listener numbers were down from previous years. The trend in the game continues to be more of just home runs, strikeouts, and walks, and more and more injuries seem to keep key players out of action.

I was going to be happy for whoever won and deserved to win the World Series in 2021.

Brian Snitker is a first-class man. A strong devotee of my former pitching coach Johnny Sain, he is a lifetime Atlanta Brave, and the World Series title is a wonderful addition to his resume. But I also *love* Dusty Baker. We have been friends, opponents, colleagues for more than 50 years. When I was with the St. Louis Cardinals on September 5, 1981 and he was with the Los Angeles Dodgers, he took me deep for a walk-off home run to deep left field in the bottom of the 11th inning. He enjoys telling me how he was sick and told Tommy Lasorda he couldn't start that day, and Lasorda told him: "Be ready. I'm going to use you for an at-bat at some point." Beware of the sick athlete. He led off the inning and hit the first pitch out for a game winner.

Baker is a Hall of Famer person and manager. He is such a humble and grateful man and respectful of the game and the way he was raised. His faith and spiritual side come through loud and clear in conversations.

The postseason games pointed out the new way the game is being played with the influence of non-playing scientists who have apparently earned the credibility of ownership to dictate to managers how games should be managed. The three dominant outcomes of an at-bat have been well documented for a few years now. Baseball has undergone many changes over the years, but this era is a major sea change! The reason for this is the information handed down by the scientists that it is easier to score a run by trying to hit high fly balls with every swing and hope that one of them goes over the fence as opposed to putting together singles, stolen bases, or sacrifice flies to score a run. It's hard to argue with it, but it has made the game less appealing to many because of the length of today's games without any action. Perhaps a double or triple could be suggested.

Every pitch today is thrown trying for a swing and miss and not soft contact. Every swing is designed to launch the ball in the air. Evidence of that is when you watch batters swing today, it defies what we were taught: *never let the barrel of the bat below the flight of the ball*. This is the opinion of excellent hitters in my era like Ted Simmons, Rod Carew, Tony Oliva, Mike Schmidt, and many more. Today, the back shoulder drops, and the barrel drops. If contact is made, it has a lot of backspin and helps the ball carry. If a player gets 550 to 600 plate appearances in a season and hits 50 percent fly balls, the statistics say 8 percent of them will clear the fence. That could be 25 home runs a year and a big contract.

Many teams cycle through three dozen pitchers in the course of a season. A 162-game season will have over 1,450 innings per team. If you keep three dozen pitchers healthy and shuttle them up and down through the course of a season, each pitcher could pitch fewer than 50 innings a season for all the innings required. Simmons pointed this plan out to me. Sad and sickening for me to think this way, but watching the World Series gives you a glimpse of the direction the game is going. I was one of the starting pitchers in the 1965 World Series, which was the last World Series where every win was a complete game by the starters. Sandy Koufax had two, Mudcat Grant had two, and Claude Osteen, Don Drysdale, and I each had one.

It is efficient for teams but not appealing to me as a fan. Since all World Series games start after 8:00 PM and last three-and-a-half to four hours, I have a new way to watch them. I might watch the first couple innings. Then I hit the record button. Early the next morning before I check the results, I watch the recording. I keep my eyes on the low right corner of the TV screen. If I see the indication there are men on base and the score might change, I watch it. I can catch the 20 minutes or so of drama and eliminate the full counts and lack of balls being put in play. I love the intensity and drama of these games, but I don't have the patience to endure long periods of time with no action. I hope I'm in the minority, and today's fans can tolerate that. The game needs them. Attendance and TV rating are down.

Before Game Five of the World Series, I texted my former Cardinals teammate John Stuper, the current head baseball coach at Yale, with my thoughts on starting Tucker Davidson in Game Five. I always respect the people who make these decisions because they know their personnel better than I do. But I do have opinions on those decisions. I thought coming off an ineffective start in Houston that Max Fried would have been the best choice to start Game Five. I think his stuff and his control would have been sharper. By starting Davidson, the Braves gave the Astros hope. He is inexperienced and looked noticeably uncomfortable.

Regardless, everyone in Atlanta is thrilled with how it turned out. Freddie Freeman has a ring. Snitker is rewarded for his loyalty to the Braves organization, and the organization was rewarded for its loyalty to him. I am certainly happy for him. I still have a hole in my baseball heart for Baker. He has had a very successful career as a manager but no World Series ring. Cito Gaston has two rings and is not in the Hall of Fame. I hope the Hall of Fame soon inducts them both. They are deserving.

I was impressed by the way Fried bounced back from his ineffective postseason starts. Getting his ankle stepped on in the first inning and avoiding injury seemed to light a spark. You could see it in his eyes. If he allowed a couple runs in that first inning, the crowd would have ignited the Astros. But he shut them down, and the crowd never had reason to get amped up. To me, that was the turning point of the game. Some people don't think a turning point in a game can happen in the first inning, but it can. I have pitched many games where escaping damage in the first turned the game around for our team

There are still a lot of questions floating around about the lack of action, length of games, and overspecialization of using pitchers. I hope the folks in charge find a way to make regular-season games more appealing and played at a faster pace. The negatives of the game have been kicked around for several years now. The game needs a more positive vibe.

Acknowledgments

Among the many people who were instrumental in so many ways who have allowed me to be a part of this great game for 62 seasons, touching eight different decades: John Kaat, Bob Hoover, Bobby Shantz, Jack McKeon, Eddie Lopat, Johnny Sain, Chuck Tanner, Tim McCarver, Bill White, Mike McCarthy, Russ Gabay, Tony Petitti, Bob Costas, and Sandy Montag. I'm sure I've missed a few and I apologize.

—J.K.

This book would not have been possible if I had not met Jim Kaat through my brother, Jeffrey, and my good friend, Joe Castiglione. Thank you. My thanks also to Cassidy Lent, manager of reference services at the National Baseball Hall of Fame.

—D.L.

About the Authors

Jim Kaat was a major league pitcher for 25 seasons (1959–1983) with the original Washington Senators, Minnesota Twins, Chicago White Sox, Philadelphia Phillies, New York Yankees, and St. Louis Cardinals. He was the pitching coach for the Cincinnati Reds from 1984 to 1985. Since then he has been an analyst for the Twins, the Yankees, CBS, ESPN, TBS, and MLB Network. He is the coauthor of *Winning Baseball— Science and Strategies* with Daryl Siedentop, the coauthor of *Still Pitching* with Phil Pepe, and the coauthor of *If These Walls Could Talk: The New York Yankees* with Greg Jennings.

Douglas Lyons is a criminal lawyer in New York City. He is the coauthor of *Out of Left Field, Short Hops, and Foul Tips* and *Curveballs and Screwballs* with his brother Jeffrey; *From an Orphan to a King* with Eddie and Anne Marie Feigner; *Broadcast Rite and Sites: I Saw It on the Radio* with the Boston Red Sox and *Can You Believe It?* with Joe Castiglione; *Catching Heat: the Jim Leyritz Story* with Jeffrey Lyons and Jim Leyrtiz; and on his own: *Baseball—A Geek's Bible, The Baseball Geek's Bible, American History: A Geek's Bible, 100 Years of Who's Who in Baseball*, and *The New York Yankees Home Run Almanac*.